REAL ESTATE
REVOLUTION

REAL ESTATE REVOLUTION
Who Will Survive?

by
Thomas Ervin

NOTTINGHAM PRESS
P.O. Box 1090/Birmingham, Michigan 48012

To my wife, Nancy
and our children,
Patrick, Timothy, William,
Daniel, Sarah, and Lynn Sue

TABLE OF CONTENTS

7

PREFACE

From time to time, various articles appear in different publications announcing the entry of another giant corporation into the real estate business or a related field.

Most people active in the real estate business have heard and/or seen recent indications that changes are indeed rampant and far reaching. Yet, only sketchy information and unrelated facts have been available, thus far.

This book has been compiled in an attempt to lay out the facts, clarify the *real issues,* and suggest possible alternatives for today's Realtor.

Much of the information has been provided by some of the corporations mentioned in the book; other portions are the result of published documents and first hand experience the author obtained from a varied real estate background.

ACKNOWLEDGMENTS

Mr. Charles Atwood, President, Merrill Lynch Realty Associates, Inc.

Mr. Cliff Bowman, Director, Marketing & Public Relations Services, A. E. LePage, Limited

Ms. Karen Brown, Merrill Lynch Relocation Management Company

Mrs. Beverly Dordick, Librarian, National Association of Realtors

Mr. Donald Hart, Vice President, Account Services, Simons Michelson Zieve, Inc., Advertising

Mr. Earl G. Keim, Jr., Chairman, The Keim Group, Limited

Mr. Walter Kiernan, Manager, Marketing & Communications, Merrill Lynch Relocation Management Company

Mr. Walter Kowal, Director of Real Estate, Continental Restaurant Systems

Mr. Frederick Pelloni, Treasurer, The Keim Group, Limited

Mr. David Simkins, Vice President, Earl Keim Realty, Inc.

A DEFINITION

Revolution:
A total or radical change

INTRODUCTION

The giants have come to the real estate business! Once dominated by small businesses, the real estate industry is literally being invaded by multi-million dollar corporations on every level.

Are these statements an over exaggeration of fact made by an eager author too anxious to sell a book? What are the facts that support this bold proclamation?

Often rumored and long awaited, national real estate brokerage firms are being formed right now. The current leader, Coldwell Banker Company of Los Angeles, on March 1, 1979, had 165 residential offices and 35 commercial offices and staff of 7,100 people.[8, 13]

Merrill Lynch, a name familiar to most Americans, announced in the September 22, 1978, issue of the *Wall Street Journal* that a new subsidiary was being formed.[20] This new entity, entitled Merrill Lynch Realty Associates, planned to enter the residential broker business by acquiring existing companies around the country.

Large firms are active elsewhere in the real estate industry. Sears and Roebuck acquired a third party purchase company. Fifty percent of this company,[21] named Executrans, was later sold to Coldwell Banker Company forming a partnership between the nation's largest Realtor* and largest retailer.

Also active in the third party purchase field are Merrill Lynch with the acquisition of TICOR Relocation Management Company, Homequity, Inc., and Control Data Corporation with its subsidiary, Residential Relocation Services and many others.

In the MLS computer field, the corporate giants are numerous. Four companies, all privately held, have been acquired by such names as: McGraw Hill, Moore Business Forms, Inc., Planning Research, and The American Broadcasting Company.

Home warranty services, sometimes maligned and often misunderstood, are definitely here to stay. Now being sold by franchisees and independent Realtors, warranty sales have skyrocketed. Following the success of the well-known H.O.W. program in the new home sales, used home warranties are in demand by today's home buyers and sellers.

The dynamic growth of real estate franchising, both nationally and regionally, is familiar to everyone in the real estate business. Although still a relatively new concept, its overwhelming success stories are sufficient enough to guarantee its continued growth in the future. Sometimes conceived as appealing to weak firms only, it is attracting a growing legion of good, well-founded companies.

In the midst of all these changes, our clients are also in the process of change. They are more knowledgable about values and the whole home buying process. Bombarded by mass media advertising, buyers are being sold on the benefits

---

*The term "Realtor" is a registered trademark of the National Association of Realtors.

of bigness. No longer interested in only an appraisal, today's home seller is comparing the services available from each Realtor.

Where will you and your company be in the 1980s? Your competition in the next five years will be much different than any that you have faced until now! How will you react to the changes mentioned in the preceding paragraphs? Will you ignore them? Do you understand them? Do you have enough present facts on which to base future decisions? Do you know what your alternatives are?

The purpose of this book is threefold:

1) To tell you what is happening
2) To show how these changes will affect you
3) To suggest alternatives for you

Each chapter will highlight a particular trend; show you the facts; and summarize by explaining its impact on you. As a result of reading this book, you will have information that will help you know:

• How the new national real estate companies are being formed and their potential appeal to the buying and selling public.

• The services available from national companies and your necessary response.

• The market impact and control exerted by third party companies in the transferee market.

• Requirements of a Realtor desirous of third party patronage.

• The role and the services offered by computer service companies.

• The features that make for a successful home warranty program.

• The growing trend toward increased use of warranty programs and the reasons behind it.

• How to compare one real estate franchise with another.

17

- The necessary ingredients of a long range successful real estate franchise relationship.
- Our changing clientele and what they are looking for.
- Your future and your alternatives in light of these many new changes.

As you can see even by these opening remarks, the advent of big business in real estate is changing the balance of power from the many to the few. This book is intended to help you understand these changes and prepare you for the challenges ahead.

1 TODAY'S MARKET PLACE

The best investment available in America today is the single family home. Stories of wildfire inflation and the realization of huge profits in home sales are commonplace. The real tax advantages, coupled with the natural pride of ownership, have led buyers into Realtors'* offices in record numbers. The average Realtor today is enjoying a prosperity never before seen on such a wide scale.

A real estate status report, prepared by the Department of Economics and Research of the National Association of Realtors, says in part: "The National Association of Realtors shared in this boom as its membership jumped from just under 400,000 in mid-1975 to nearly 640,000 in mid-1978. The median income of male brokers was $30,000 with the typical earnings of their female counterparts at $19,500. The median gross income of full time salesmen

---

*The term "Realtor" is a registered trademark of the National Association of Realtors.

was $17,000 versus a median of $12,000 for full time saleswomen."[19]

Commission income, a function of property value, has risen with the high rate of inflation experienced in recent years. *This huge dollar volume of commission income has not gone unnoticed by big business.*

In a very methodical way, typical of big business, national real estate companies are beginning to emerge in various segments of our industry. Some of these companies and developments are familiar to you and others are not.

NATIONAL BROKERAGE FIRMS

A national brokerage firm is a large real estate company operating in numerous states with branch offices that are owned and operated as a single company.

The age of the national company is now upon us. Rumors have pervaded national Realtor conventions for many years. The thought of a national retail organization entering our field, such as Sears, has cast fear into the hearts and minds of most Realtors. Many of us have envisioned how such an invasion would occur. From some of the facts now available, the trends appear obvious.

A case in point is the A. E. LePage Group of Companies with corporate offices in Toronto, Canada. A. E. LePage, Limited was founded in 1913, by Albert Edward LePage.[6] It is the largest real estate company in Canada. The company is comprised of approximately 177 offices and 3,000 people including salespeople and administrative personnel. One of the many LePage divisions is a national referral organization entitled Coast-to-Coast Real Estate Service. Another 190 independent brokerage firms across Canada join the 177 LePage offices to comprise the total of approximately 367 offices in Coast-to-Coast.

Additional services provided by other LePage divisions are: appraisal and consulting, commercial development, industrial sales and leasing, investment property sales, mortgage financing, office leasing, property management, re-search, planning and feasability studies, and shopping center development. It is the author's opinion that the A. E. LePage Company is the model of the type of national real estate company that is emerging in the United States. The huge volume of residential brokerage business written from a national network of offices justifies the profitable formation of all the other services mentioned above. The A. E. LePage Company is practically self-sustaining in that it is not reliant on many other outside entities to provide its services. With ownership of a national referral organization, a mortgage division, advertising and public relations divisions, full time trainers, and specialists in other support activities, LePage can bring enormous competitive advantages to the marketplace.

The largest real estate company in the United States today is Coldwell-Banker Company, headquartered in Los Angeles. "Founded in 1906 by Colbert Coldwell, the company seven years later was joined by Benjamin A. Banker. Beginning primarily with a base of commercial brokerages, Coldwell-Banker has initiated and sustained a very ambitious acquisition program that encompasses all phases of the real estate business."[6]

As of March 1, 1979, Coldwell-Banker had 165 residential brokerage offices and 7,100 people including sales and administrative personnel.[13]

The 1978 annual report reveals that gross revenues from all divisions was $204,811,000 with 41% or $84,000,000 coming from the Residential Brokerage Company. The commercial brokerage division contributed $89,000,000 or 43% of gross revenue. Some of the other revenue is obtained in the form of escrow fees, insurance commissions, mortgage loan fees, property management fees, development services, consultation and appraisal fees.[8]

In addition to acquiring residential brokerages, Coldwell-Banker has taken the initiative in other related areas. On November 15, 1977, 99.3% of Nationwide Find-a-

Home Service, Inc. was added to the Coldwell collection. Nationwide is a 600 company national referral service reputed to be one of the finest and most extensive in the United States. This move gives Coldwell-Banker a Realtor network similar to the Coast-to-Coast network of A. E. Le-Page in Canada.

In startling rapidity, an agreement dated January, 16, 1978, was made with Coast-to-Coast whereby Nationwide and Coast-to-Coast members would begin to exchange clients across the American-Canadian border. This established, in effect, the largest referral organization in North America.[6] This move had another effect of combining the talents and resources of the two largest residential brokerages in North America, A. E. LePage and Coldwell-Banker.

Another national real estate company is in the making under the guidance of the Merrill Lynch ("Bullish on America") Company. The new company, Merrill Lynch Realty Associates, has corporate offices in Stamford, Connecticut. It was also revealed that talks are ongoing with real estate companies for their possible acquisition. With the uncertainty and volatility of the stock brokerage business, it would seem that real estate brokerage would be a natural for a company dependent on commission income and knowledgeable in various other fields of investment services.

RELOCATION COMPANIES

Let us leave the topic of national real estate companies momentarily and investigate the third party purchase companies. A third party company enlists a corporation in a contractual arrangement whereby the third party company aids its transferring employee by giving him his entire equity in his home based on competent appraisals. This enables the employee to move on to his new home without actually putting his existing home up for sale. Once the third party company takes ownership of the property, a Realtor is selected to handle the sale. Sears and Roebuck,

Inc., long rumored as a possible entrant into the real estate industry, acquired Executrans, Inc. Executrans, like the familiar Home Equity Company, is one of the leaders in the third party field. Although not in the brokerage business yet, this marked the first time that a national retailer became involved in a real estate oriented business.

Sears did not wait long before establishing a deeper penetration into our business. On July 26, 1978, an announcement was made by Coldwell-Banker. A mailgram was sent out to Nationwide members which said in part: "Coldwell-Banker, the parent firm of Nationwide Find-a-Home, announced today that it had agreed in principle to purchase a 50% equity interest in Executrans, Inc. from Allstate Enterprises, Inc., a wholly owned subsidiary of Sears Roebuck and Company. . . ."[21] This Executrans deal was a departure from the typical Coldwell-Banker style. It was a stock transaction which gave 43,333 shares of Coldwell stock to Sears.[8] The purchase of businesses in the past had been accomplished with cash. It also established a partnership in that neither party had controlling interest in Executrans.

This development now engages Coldwell Banker in joint venture type relationships with the largest retailer in the U.S. and the largest real estate company in Canada, A. E. LePage, Ltd. *This new combination of giants will have far-reaching effects on the way real estate is sold in the future!*

Early in 1977, Merrill Lynch and Company also entered the third party field with the acquisition of TICOR Relocation Management Company. This entity was purchased from the huge Title Insurance Company of California. Shortly after the acquisition, Merrill Lynch introduced a new concept in choosing Realtors in each market. Traditionally, a third party company would work with numerous Realtors in each market. The theory was to keep all Realtors on their toes by giving them a listing from time to time. You could be passed over for future listings if previous properties were mishandled.

The Merrill Lynch approach was quite different in design. Only one company in each major market was selected. Interviews were conducted with the larger firms and a decision was made on a market by market basis. A condition of the Merrill Lynch appointment stipulated that all managers of the selected Realtor, at their own expense, must go through their broker certification program. This entailed a full week spent at a selected Merrill Lynch training facility. A test was given and future training was mentioned as conditional to maintaining the certified broker status. In return, all Merrill Lynch listings were given only to the designated broker in each market. It was obviously felt that greater leverage could be exerted on a Realtor by offering all leads in his town or losing everything by nonconformance to their requirements. After approximately 19 months in the third party business, Merrill Lynch decided to enter the brokerage business as previously stated. The companies, who are negotiating with Merrill Lynch Realty Associates for acquisition, are most probably in those markets now servicing the Merrill Lynch third party corporate accounts and now in their broker certification program.

There are, of course, other large companies in the third party purchase business such as Homequity, a name familiar to most Realtors.

Most third party companies charge an all-encompassing commission rate which includes all costs to be encountered in the purchase and disposal of a transferee's home. A typical percentage would be 17% of the purchase price of the home. Out of this would come the Realtor's commission, interest expense on equity paid to the transferee, management costs. maintenance costs and others.

A startling fact recently revealed in a survey of Fortune's top 1,000 companies, was that 45% of all corporations surveyed now use the services of a third party company.[18] This means in effect, that a large percentage of the transferee market is controlled by these third party companies and not available to the average Realtor who does not enjoy their patronage. In other words, your best friend could be helpless in attempting to give you the listing on his home if a third party company is involved in his move.

COMPUTER SERVICE COMPANIES

Another rapidly growing area is the real estate computer service industry. This service virtually had its debut in late 1967. On November 11, 1967, a computer located in Detroit answered telephone inquiries from the National Realtor Convention in Washington, D.C. Mr. Jack Jominy, now president of Realtron Corporation and previously executive vice president of the Western Wayne-Oakland County Board of Realtors, introduced this new concept to many Realtors in attendance. The computer stored each property currently listed and all properties sold in the preceding twelve months. By inserting price, area, and features through a touch tone telephone the computer would search its files in thousandths of a second and formulate a voice message back to the inquiring party.

In the years 1967-1970, Realtors nationwide were installing computer systems in their multiple listing services at a maddening pace. As in the brokerage business, the real estate computer services have attracted some of the giants of industry.

International Graphics Corp., a computer and printing services company was recently acquired by the Moore Business Forms Company. Realtronics, formerly privately held, is now owned by the large and diversified Planning Research, Inc. of McLean, Virginia. Another service company, Multi-List, Inc., of Denver, Atlanta, and San Antonio, was the recent acquisition of the well-known publishing company, McGraw Hill. The R. L. White company of Louisville, Kentucky was purchased by ABC. The one privately held company left among the giants is Realtron Corporation of Detroit, with printing plants in Michigan, Massachusetts, and Florida.

A great variety of services are being offered the Realtor today including weekly picture books showing all homes currently listed in a particular MLS, talking and printing computers accessible by telephone, statistical reports, comparable sales books showing recent sales for appraisal purposes, broker accounting, investment analysis programs, and others soon to be announced. With the rapid turnover in property, computers have enabled their users to keep pace and know about their competitors' listings quickly. If business slows and the level of listings available increases, the computer eliminates much necessary record keeping by zeroing in on the kind of property specifically required.

Unlike the giant companies that are going into competition with today's broker, these companies bring services designed to preserve the continuity of each broker, large and small. They are investing millions of dollars in plant and equipment. Because computer services are available through the multiple listing structure, they are sold to all members on an equal basis. As a multiple listing service grows and its members become increasingly successful, the computer companies benefit in direct proportion. If huge national real estate companies could eventually force many smaller companies out of business, the computer companies would lose their greatest source of revenue. Fortunately, then, the small broker has allies in his local real estate board, its MLS organization, and the computer company that services it.

HOME WARRANTY SERVICES

The next topic is quite misunderstood by most real estate salespeople today. The topic is the home warranty industry. Palace Guard, the acknowledged pioneer in this field, went bankrupt. The Realtors around the country, who were Palace Guard brokers had to step in and underwrite the existing warranties in effect against claims until their terms expired. The bankruptcy occurred in the mid-1970s.

Four years later, many of those original Palace Guard Realtors are continuing to provide warranty protection for their clients. Although Palace Guard has left the scene, the service lingers on. In fact, the concept is alive and thriving!

The reputed leader in warranty sales nationally is American Home Shield of Pleasanton, California. This company claims control of 60% of all warranties sold nationally. It also underwrites and services some warranty programs sold by national real estate franchises under different names.

In those companies offering warranties, most salespeople are still not as enthusiastic as their brokers seem to be. This is possibly due to the bankruptcy of Palace Guard, a lack of knowledge of the true value of the service to home buyers and sellers, a feeling that the coverage is not complete enough, and a natural reluctance to sell a concept that they neither understand or believe.

The author is a firm believer in the necessity of the home warranty concept. Our clients need this service and it should be made available within the real estate industry rather than from without! It provides another reason to deal with a Realtor. In these times of increasing "for sale by owners," it is important to have another service that the owner cannot offer.

There are two other considerations: First, consumerism is rampant. Every product and service being offered today must have the safety and well being of the consumer in mind. The Realtor asks people to make the largest investment of their lives in a product that has been previously owned, that is 10-50 years old, with a heating system, cooling system, electric system, plumbing system, and various appliances. If today's consumers can receive a warranty on a car tire, wristwatch, or used car, why can't one be found for a used house? Now, when our customers move into a home, they have no one to turn to.

The warranty company steps in just as the seller and Realtor step out to provide ongoing service after the sale. This brings up a second reason for the guaranteed future of

29

the warranty concept. There is proposed legislation in state and national legislative committees that will invalidate the "as is" clause in our purchase agreements and put the liability for problems found subsequent to occupancy squarely in the laps of our sellers. It would not be surprising if some of the liability would be also spread to the broker or brokers who were parties to the transaction. As you are probably aware, the HOW warranty program now available in the sale of new homes is meeting with increased success and record numbers of warranties offered each year. If a warranty is necessary on a home that is brand-new, is it not therefore doubly important on a used home?

FRANCHISES

A real estate franchisor is a company that enters into a contractual arrangement with real estate brokerages. This contract calls for the provision of various services that are to be provided to the broker in return for an initial fee and an ongoing percentage of the broker's gross income.

By this time you probably have some feelings about real estate franchises. Here is an interesting quotation from that same study undertaken by the Department of Economics and Research of the National Association of Realtors dated September, 1978: "The growing national trend toward franchising was evident in our survey. Overall, 17.1% of the brokers were affiliated with a franchise firm, compared to just 8.5% three years earlier. Interestingly enough, the median income of brokers in non-franchised firms ($30,000) continues to be higher than their franchised counterparts ($24,000)."[17]

This tells us that the number of brokers buying franchises has doubled while the type of broker joining franchises is in an income group less than average.

The author has operated as an independent broker, as a franchisee, and now serves in the capacity of a franchisor. He has some very definite and strong feelings on how a franchisor should serve his clients and the ground rules under which his services should be sold.

If you as an entrepreneur and owner of your own business want to successfully compete in the environment described thus far in this opening chapter, you are going to need some first rate professional help. The environment in which you have been able to bring your business to its present status is changing more rapidly than you know. The old time proven solutions will not serve tomorrow's problems.

A real full-service franchise should have the following attributes: The name and corporate logo should be easily recognized; a franchisee should have some definite degree of exclusivity so that he knows another franchise will not be sold across the street; the local Realtor name should be continued in a prominent manner so that he doesn't completely abandon a name familiar to the community in which he operates; the franchisor must have a competent staff with an advertising department, a corporate relocation department, training department offering both sales and management training programs, a good, well managed home warranty service, professional and periodic consulting on all phases of the brokerage business; a national referral network that really has broad coverage and is fairly administered.

A franchise concept must allow for a certain density of offices so that a synergistic effect may be created. The dictionary defines synergism as, "the co-operative action of two agencies such that the total effect is greater than the sum of the two effects taken independently."[23]

Many brokers question the benefits that are really derived from affiliating with a franchise. One comment often heard is that the success of any company is dependent on the effort put forth by its broker and sales staff. Joining a franchise does not diminish the need for continued effort. However, the concept of the synergistic effect dictates that the efforts of numerous brokers, all with the same identity, will generate far greater results than if a common identity was not shared by all.

You benefit every time another member of your franchise puts up a for sale sign, runs an ad, opens an office, or does anything that promotes your common name to the public. Two brokers in the same franchise should more than double the impact on their market versus when they competed against one another separately. Do not ignore or overlook the power of the synergistic effect when considering franchising.

Here is a final thought on franchising. A franchisor must design his pricing structure and services rendered so that the cost versus benefits comparison will lead to the financial security of each franchisee. There will be much more on the pros and cons of franchises later.

OUR CHANGING CLIENTELE

Something else is changing in our business. Our buyers and sellers are changing. A recent statistic stated that 88% of all home buyers today have already owned a previous home. Buyers are more knowledgeable today. As people live in a home a shorter period of time, they move more often and are therefore more in touch with values, financing, closing, negotiating, and other facets.

With the great communication explosion, clients are more aware of your competitors and all the other options open to them in the selection of a new home. Sellers also have matured and have become more selective in choosing a listing agent. In addition to an opinion of value, they want to compare services so as to gain the most benefits possible from their listing agent.

Most people today have some idea of the value of their home and MLS enables most competitors to appraise a property quite closely by using many of the same comparable sales statistics. The real competition, then, gets down to image, services, professionalism, both product and institutional advertising program, and the particular expertise and training of the sales associates involved.

We have all learned that past loyalties and personal ties are not as strong as they once were. The American buying public has demonstrated a trait of patronizing big name businesses. Bigness has been sold to us as being synonymous with quality, reliability, consistency, and a certain sameness that generates a feeling of well being. By and large, it is fair to say that the big get bigger and the small try to get bigger.

Things are often more believable when we can relate to them personally. Let us look at the MLS of which you are a member. Take a copy of the roster of each office in your MLS. If your current listings are printed in a book, take out a sheet of paper and make a mark on the paper for each listing in the book that is listed by an office of a large company or a member of a franchise. If your MLS prints the listings on separate sheets, just put each listing of a large office or franchisee in one stack. Tally the total of all MLS current listings and the total of these listed by a large office or franchisee. The number of listings per office for the larger offices and franchisees will be significantly higher than the average.

Now remember that the figures just calculated are prior to the entry of national real estate companies into your market. Where will their listings come from? Naturally, they will come in varying degrees from all brokers currently in your market. The brokers who stand to lose the most listings are those who are ill equipped to offer the services available from the large companies and the franchises.

It would appear that now is the time to begin thinking about these things. Too many of us run our brokerages by accident rather than on purpose! We don't act in advance of a coming event often enough. Changes are not only coming; they are upon us and are increasing at a dizzying pace.

You have now read about national real estate brokerages in the making, the power and influence of third party companies, national computer service companies, home warranty services, real estate franchises, and the changing buyers and sellers that we must serve.

Before we go any further, let's talk about you. Where are you going? Have you given any thought to what your future will be in the real estate field? One of the purposes of this book is to enable you to escape the day to day crises of the sales business and take a good look down the road ahead of you.

Are you a salesperson who has just opened your own brokerage? Are you planning on retiring from the real estate business and selling your business? Do you plan to leave your business to a successor such as a son or trusted manager or other employee? Does a partner seem attractive to you? Do you plan to enlarge your staff and number of offices? Are you comfortable with a small business but want very much to remain in the real estate business for a long time? Are you already very large but find that you don't have good control of your business?

Do you establish goals for your business at the beginning of each year? Do you relate these goals to an annual budget? Do you know what the goals of your salespeople are? Do you have a goal? Do they know what the company goals are? Do you know how your listing volume in number of units compares with last year at this time? How does your percent of sales volume to the total MLS compare with last year? Are you going forward or backward? What degree of public recognition do you enjoy in your marketplace? Why should a salesman come to work for you rather than the company down the street? What kind of connections do you have nationally? What services can you offer a seller that your competitors cannot? What kind of budget have you established for institutional advertising? What co-ordinated plan do you have to obtain corporate clients? What plans do you have to systematically keep in touch with past clients? Before you opened your present office or offices, did you do any research to determine the feasibility of your potential success?

If you can answer the majority of those questions in the affirmative, you are thinking like a big businessman. If you don't know the answer to most of the questions, then you may be running your business like the typical salesman who happens to own a business.

Most brokers today were good salesmen with other companies who decided to go it on their own. Even though you now own a real estate company, you might still be thinking like a salesman. The next listing and next sale and definitely the next closing take up all your conscious thoughts.

You don't have the liberty to own a business and think like a salesman! Continue to sell, but think like an owner of a business. Think about the next listing, sale and closing, but think about the future too. *Decide your* future yourself. Don't let fate decide it for you.

ALTERNATIVES

You will need professional advisors in different areas of management and marketing to effectively compete with the coming competition. There are basically three directions that are available to you:

1. *Remain An Independent Broker* and gather what services you can from your local MLS and real estate board. Services not obtainable there may be found in the business sector. Example: some computer, training, and MLS services are available through the local board of Realtors. A national referral service, home warranty program, advertising and management consulting may be found elsewhere.

2. *Acquire Or be Acquired* so that the gross revenues will be large enough to build a staff of competent specialists in training, advertising, and other services. Some large

real estate companies have full time people handling each of these categories. Example: A large Realtor in the Midwest has a full time advertising person who co-ordinates both institutional (radio and TV) and day to day newspaper insertions which usually include some message about a particular service in addition to highlighting a certain number of properties. A full time director is responsible for training of sales associates and ongoing programs for management enhancement. One person handles all physical problems of plant and equipment. Two attorneys handle all closings personally. One man handles all trades and guarantees. A corporate relocation department has been established with a dedicated staff. One person works on site selection for expansion purposes and handles the renewal of leases on existing locations.

Being acquired has the obvious disadvantage of taking away your autonomy as an independent businessman. If someone is willing to purchase your company as part of an expansion program, they want to see their new acquisition perform well. Some of their methods may be the opposite of yours. It may also be the opportunity for you to grow as a businessman and be a part of a larger more successful entity than the business you once had. As the years go by, there can be advancement opportunities that can take you to greater heights than you could have ever reached in your own business.

3. *Buy a Real Estate Franchise* and remain the owner of your company. If the franchise you choose is a full service franchise with a competent staff, you should expect and receive all the services mentioned previously in the franchising discussion.

This concludes an opening overview of the events taking place today and the options open to you. In each subsequent chapter, you will probe these developments in more depth and study some conclusions on how they will affect you.

2 NATIONAL BROKERAGE FIRMS

Look at the following facts! Listed on the New York Stock Exchange; 200 offices in fourteen states; 7,100 people in the organization; 205 million dollars in commissions and fees; 38 million dollars in ready cash; history of buying large competitors with cash; international business and financial connections; a conglomerate with ownership of many affiliated type businesses; partnership with the largest retailer in the United States; national goals of market domination. [8]

What kind of company is this? What industry is it in? Insurance, Banking, Title Insurance, Construction? Unbelievable as it may seem, this is a real estate brokerage firm! Although practically unknown by the average working broker today, the giant Coldwell Banker Company of California, is amassing the largest national network of wholly owned real estate brokerage firms ever seen!

Is it possible that today's Realtor has never even heard of the largest company in his industry? Most people in other industries know which companies are in the leadership positions. Ask an insurance man about the largest insurance company in the U.S. He'll know. The next time you talk to your accountant, ask him about his competition. He'll know their size, structure, and current posture in the marketplace.

Ask a Realtor if he has heard of Coldwell Banker or A. E. LePage, Limited. He probably hasn't. He will not have heard of the two largest real estate brokerage firms in North America. Why is this? What does it tell us about the real estate industry as it exists today?

To understand our industry, we must first look at the people in it. What is the profile of the average real estate broker? He or she is probably someone who has never worked for major corporations or is an escapee from some giant company who wanted the life of the small independent businessman. The attractiveness of being your own boss, making an unlimited income, starting a business with relatively low initial investment, and making an impact on the local community have traditionally been some of the inducements of real estate sales.

All brokers and owners of residential brokerage firms were good salesmen working for another broker at some point in time. For many varying reasons, the day came when it seemed right to go it on their own. Now the typical day is spent trying to get that next listing, next offer, next closing, and next good salesperson. Not having had much formal management training, today's broker still thinks much like a salesman.

Goal setting, budgeting, market analysis, staff enhancement, and such like terms are basically unknown or at least unused concepts in far too many brokerages today. Particularly with the great real estate market enjoyed in 1977, and 1978, most brokers have been hard pressed to handle the tremendous volume of business that has come their way.

In the midst of this recent success, the growth of franchises has been noticed by most brokers. With mixed reactions, the independent broker will concede that changes are taking place in the competitive balance between companies in each market.

The changes evoked by national real estate companies, however, will be much more traumatic than those of the franchises. After all, you can always join a franchise if you are so disposed. When a national company acquires a fellow Realtor in your town, you have no choice but to compete with them as effectively as you can.

Let us go back in history for a moment to 1913. Mr. Colbert Coldwell and Benjamin Banker were little known real estate entrepreneurs in California. In that same year, Albert LePage was entering into a similar business in Toronto, Canada. Through the years they worked diligently to build their budding businesses into solid companies.

Today, 65 years later, these two businesses have reached the pinnacle in their chosen profession! Mr. Coldwell and Mr. Banker's company is the largest real estate brokerage firm in the United States with 200 offices and[8] 7,100 people in sales and service capacities. The entity begun by Mr. LePage is the largest real estate company in Canada. With 177 offices[6] and 3,300 people, it is the first prototype of a new concept in real estate sales. *It is the first national real estate company!*

Both of these companies today are corporate giants in every sense of the word. Diversified, well financed, professionally managed, aggressively led, they are showing us the wave of the future in real estate sales. No longer a rumor or mere conjecture, the national real estate company is a reality. And these giants are seeking domination of the marketplace wherever they go. Through acquisitions and mergers, their growth rate in the last 10 years has been meteoric.

Both companies grew separately in their own areas but with a respect for the accomplishments of each other. Then the inevitable happened! They began to work more closely with one another and developments in 1977 and 1978, have been quite astounding. In August of 1977, A. E. LePage, Limited, purchased 150,000 shares of Coldwell Banker and Company stock valued at that time at 2.5 million dollars. This gave them a 7% ownership position in Coldwell Banker. It also gave them their first big investment in the U.S. Officials of A.E. LePage, Limited, explained it this way; "While considering the invasion of the U.S. market, there were three ways we could go. One method would have been the outright acquisition of one or more established brokerage companies—the same as we have done in Canada. The other alternatives we considered were, opening our own U.S. offices, or acquiring an interest in a major U.S. broker."[5]

Mr. Gordon C. Gray (Chairman of A.E. LePage, Limited) said, "The acquisition alternative was discarded because it would have involved significant goodwill costs and would have required a major diversion of management talent for A.E. LePage executives. Opening our own offices down there (in the United States) would have resulted in an even greater diversion of management time, and would have entailed compliance with a variety of differing licensing standards in the various states.

"For these reasons, a decision was made to invest in the shares of a public U.S. real estate brokerage company, and Coldwell Banker was the vehicle chosen."

"We know them very well," Mr. Gray explained. "We've had a working association with them for many years, and I honestly believe they're the finest brokerage firm in the United States."[5]

So these two big businesses got not only bigger, but actually gravitated toward one another with representation on each others board of directors and additional interlocking arrangements.

A.E. LePAGE, LIMITED

Of the two companies, A.E. LePage, Limited, although smaller in sales volume, has gone further towards establishing a national network of offices in Canada than Coldwell Banker has in the U.S. Its organizational structure and services are very similar to those beginning to emanate from the Coldwell Banker pattern of growth. Because the formation of national real estate companies is new to most Realtors and because its impact must be thoroughly understood, let us examine the A.E. LePage Company in some depth.

In 1977, LePage participated in some 25,000 transactions having a total dollar volume of 1.5 billion dollars in real estate sales. These transactions were rather evenly split between the commercial and residential divisions.

To understand the whole company, it seems logical to examine its many parts. The separate divisions include the residential division, the commercial division, the investment division, the office leasing division, property management, Creative Circle, Limited, research and planning division, appraisals division, shopping center division, corporate relocation service, industrial sales and leasing, mortgage and corporate financing, and the commercial development division. [4]

With the acquisition of a 17 office company in October of 1978, the LePage national network of offices reached 177 in number. [3] Like the old adage about success breeding success, LePage seems to be picking up momentum in its continuing role of real estate leader in Canada. The residential and commercial divisions provide all the services that one would expect from so vast an organization. The investment division is prepared to help both individuals and corporate clients in the proper selection, analysis, acquisition, and management of investment properties capable of producing the desired results.

A. E. LePage is the dominant broker in office leasing in the major cities across Canada. In 1977, more than 1,200 office leases were negotiated successfully ranging from one man suites to several floors in major downtown complexes.

The property management division, assisted by the latest computer technology, and staffed by full time professionals, is involved in a complete array of management services for residential and commercial income properties.

Creative Circle, Limited, is a wholly owned subsidiary specializing in promotion, advertising, public image building, and other duties generally associated with an advertising agency. These promotion-oriented services are available to various clients in the U.S. and Canada in addition to the obvious internal needs of LePage nationally.

One of the sophisticated services offered to customers, the research and planning division· has set a distinct pattern of expertise in complex design projects. Included are downtown redevelopments in Toronto and other cities, shopping centers, office parks, and industrial developments across Canada.

A separate appraisal division provides market evaluations in areas involving mortgages, capital gains, mergers, book values, insurance, assessment, taxation, arbitration hearings, sale or purchase, rental surveys, industrial and commercial lease negotiations, and feasibility analysis.

Another field requiring specialized talent is the shopping center division. Some of the services include planning, financial analysis, leasing, management, construction management, advertising and promotion, redevelopment, urban projects, corporate assistance, major retail lease negotiations, and site selection.

Both the A.E. LePage owned offices and member offices of the LePage national referral network, entitled Coast-to-Coast, handle the home sale and home purchase needs of the corporate transferee. It is this division which has a working arrangement with the national referral network (Nationwide Relocation Services, Inc.) owned by Coldwell Banker in the U.S.

With 120 people in 10 major Canadian cities, the industrial sales and leasing division satisfies the needs of locating, selling and leasing industrial properties, industrial site selection and turnkey build-to-suit packages for special purpose buildings.

Mortgage and corporate financing programs secure debt capital for land financing, construction financing, long term permanent financing and refinancing, plus corporate term financing.

Another outstanding division of LePage is the Commercial Development division providing a complete concept-to-completion capability for institutions, governments and developers wanting to create substantial commercial real estate projects. This particular division has numerous, extremely complex projects that are under its guidance from start to finish.[4]

This brief review of the various A. E. LePage divisions should give you an idea of the kinds of things that are possible with a well led national real estate company.

EXAMPLE OF A NATIONAL FIRM AT WORK

To understand how the public can be better served by national companies, let's look at the following example:

Edward Executive and his wife and family live in a lovely home in suburban Washington, D.C. Ed, an executive in middle management with a national manufacturer of computer systems, has lived in his home 5 years now. Having been given assurances by his superiors that he would not be moved again, Ed, 3 years ago, invested in a neighborhood strip store center to be used as a source of income and hedge against inflation during his retirement years.

Because he had time on the weekends and evenings, he managed the center himself, collecting the rents when due and keeping the property in good repair.

On a Monday morning, he was called into the

vice president's office to be told that he had been selected to head up a new division to be formed in Kansas City. He would be promoted to vice president and given additional fringe benefits and a substantial pay raise. He would also qualify for the officers' pension benefits which were extremely generous.

Although somewhat disappointed at the thought of moving once more, he and his family decided it was worth while to make this one last move. His company had retained Executrans, Inc., owned by Coldwell Banker and Sears, to handle the sale and disposition of the homes of top level management. Because Coldwell Banker owns half of Executrans and has offices in the Washington, D.C. area, they were selected to handle the sale.

Ed received his equity in the form of a cashier's check from Executrans ten days after being notified to handle his move. The local Coldwell Banker office listed the house and referred Ed and his family to the manager of one of their offices in Kansas City. Ed felt that he should also put the strip store up for sale because he would not be able to look after it personally.

The strip store center was listed by an office of the Coldwell Banker Commercial Brokerage Company. Besides notifying other commercial firms in the Washington, D.C. market, a copy of the listing was sent to all Coldwell Banker Commercial offices around the country.

An inquiry came from a salesman with the Coldwell Banker Commercial office in Miami. He had an investor who lived in the Miami area and was desirous of such an investment on two conditions. The investor wanted a bid from a competent property management firm in D.C., who would be responsible for the onsight management responsibility. Secondly, he would want to finance the purchase with a commercial mortgage loan.

The D.C. office of Coldwell who had the strip center

listed, contacted two sister companies, Coldwell Banker Property Management Company and Coldwell Banker Management Company which has a division specializing in commercial financing. After review by representatives of these two companies, the property management bid was drafted and the mortgage loan was granted. The purchase was consumated and Ed again received another cashier's check which represented his equity in the strip center. Needless to say, Coldwell Banker took very good care of Ed's real estate needs.

Actually, seven different Coldwell Banker companies were involved in the house and strip center deals. In chronological order, they were: Executrans Inc., the Washington D.C. residential office, the Kansas City residential office, the Washington D.C. commercial office, the Miami commercial office, the Washington property management office, and the Washington commercial mortgage division.

Although the previous example was fictitious, it illustrates in dramatic form the many services that may be coordinated on a national scale by a national real estate firm.

The self sufficiency of Coldwell Banker in this example demonstrates the tremendous potential and possible market domination that could be achieved.

COLDWELL BANKER

The Coldwell Banker Company appears to be the odds on favorite to establish the first large national real estate brokerage business in the United States.

Beginning primarily with a base of commercial brokerages, Coldwell Banker has initiated and sustained a very ambitious acquisition program that encompasses all phases of the real estate business. This company has established a pattern of purchasing the leading residential brokerage firm in major markets around the country. The Coldwell Banker Residential Brokerage Company has 35 offices.

Additional offices were added beginning with the purchase of the Forest E. Olsen Company in southern California (48 offices). Then the Routh Robbins Company in the Washington D.C. area (14 offices) was acquired followed by Hardin-Stockton in Kansas City (20 offices), Thorsen Realtors in Chicago (23 offices), and Barton & Ludwig in Atlanta (25 offices).[8]

As of March 1, 1979, Coldwell Banker has 165 residential brokerage offices, 32 commercial brokerage offices and 7,100 people including sales and administrative personnel.[13]

As previously noted by the chairman of A.E. LePage, Limited, the LePage Company investigated the possibility of opening offices in the United States. Sears has long been rumored as a possible entrant into the brokerage field. Both firms, however, seem content to invest in Coldwell Banker as their primary vehicle of service. Sears owned 12.5% of Coldwell Banker stock at the beginning of March, 1979. Later, in March, both Sears and A. E. Le-Page increased their holdings in Coldwell Banker stock to 20% apiece.

Sears still may go it alone in the brokerage business someday. But, the recent joint agreement to become partners in the ownership of Executrans, Inc., indicates that Sears gives Coldwell Banker high marks for the manner in which the broker acquisition program has been conducted thus far. *One must be impressed when the largest Realtor in Canada and the largest retailer in the U.S. decide to invest in Coldwell Banker rather than attempt to structure a national real estate company on their own!*

MERRILL LYNCH
REALTY ASSOCIATES

Another company that will have an impact on the national scene is Merrill Lynch Realty Associates of Stamford, Connecticut. The game plan of this wholly owned subsidiary of Merrill Lynch & Company is quite similar to that of Coldwell Banker.

Through acquisition of leading Realtor firms across the country, the goal is the rapid formation of a national company possibly using the name of Merrill Lynch to draw on existing consumer recognition and confidence.

These offices probably would be the recipients of buyer and listing leads given out by its sister company, Merrill Lynch Relocation Management Company.

This move into the real estate industry can put the local broker in a weakened competitive position for a number of reasons. The national name is instantly recognized and quite highly respected. The obvious financial staying power of the nation's largest stock brokerage firm can prove valuable in good times and bad. The existing connection with Merrill Lynch Relocation Management Company provides additional instant leads for any company acquired.

Merrill Lynch Realty Associates has one other advantage. Besides being recognizable, the name has always been associated with the investment business. Thousands of people turn to Merrill Lynch every day to get advice on investing in America. Because so many Americans know of the great investment potential of a single family home, doesn't it seem logical to turn to the investment expert to choose a home too? Now you can go to Merrill Lynch to invest in almost anything such as: stocks, bonds, other securities, homes, land, income property, industrial, commercial and other forms of tax sheltered investment properties.

Frankly, the timeliness of the Merrill Lynch move into real estate makes good business sense. The securities business is becoming more and more volatile as the mutual funds and other big investors make the stock market more precarious and unpredictable.

People, on the other hand, are always buying and selling homes for a myriad of reasons that are often completely unrelated to the state of the economy.

The ownership of residential real estate brokerage firms should provide a good cushion to offset the huge commitment in facilities and personnel dedicated solely to the securities business. This stabilizing factor could make the acquisition of Realtor firms more attractive in the future to other stock brokerage firms who are watching the Merrill Lynch "experiment" with keen interest.

Lastly, but perhaps most important, is the total potential income to be derived in real estate. The estimated commission income earned in real estate sales in 1978, was approximately $12 billion. The total commission income from the sale of securities was $3.7 billion. Think of it! Three times more dollars were paid to Realtors than stock brokers last year! Extra commission income and the recent IRS rule allowing the first $100,000 in home profit tax free contributed to the timing of the Merrill Lynch move.[14]

MERRILL LYNCH PLAN

This author conducted an interview with Mr. Charles Atwood, President of Merrill Lynch Realty Associates, in the beginning of February, 1979. This interview was prior to the announcement of any acquisitions of real estate firms. Mr. Atwood gave some of the following facts to clarify the anticipated future direction of his newly formed subsidiary.

It has planned on acquiring forty real estate firms by 1983. The basic formula would call for Merrill Lynch Realty Associates receiving an 80% position in the acquired firm. He felt that this would give some assurance that the principal would continue to have an active and aggressive interest in taking the company forward after the acquisition had been made. If things went well, Mr. Atwood pointed out, the 20% remaining interest could be worth more down the road than the original price for the 80% received from Merrill Lynch. If the principal of the acquired company was ready to retire shortly, the 20% could be sold to one or two key managers who would carry on the business and become an equity partner with Merrill Lynch.

Mr. Atwood said the primary reason for the formation of Merrill Lynch Realty Associates was to extend additional services to the huge customer base built up over the years by the parent company in the securities business. He said further that it was the intention of the parent company to diversify to a large enough degree so that they would become known as a large financial service company of which the stock brokerage business was a part.

When asked if the acquired firms would automatically receive business from the local Merrill Lynch Relocation Management office, he said that it was possible but that they would have to provide the level of service required or they could lose the patronage of the relocation company. He clearly made the point that all Merrill Lynch companies will have to stand on their own merits.

At the opening of the interview, he stated that the three disciplines Merrill Lynch could bring to each brokerage firm acquired were: marketing and advertising, finance and control, and training and management development. He felt that these three categories of assistance plus future linkage of the local broker's identity with that of Merrill Lynch would result in a long and profitable relationship.

The firms being sought at the outset are in the major markets around the country. In some cases, they are located in cities heavily serviced by the relocation company and also in other large cities not so serviced.

The author asked him what he would do about those secondary markets that may not have a clearly dominant brokerage firm. He did not rule out opening a real estate branch office in the facility currently used by the local Merrill Lynch stock brokerage office. He did say, however, that he did not believe those people employed in the stock brokerage office would engage in the sale of real estate.

As a past employee and one of the originators of TI-COR relocation management company, Mr. Atwood became a Merrill Lynch employee when TICOR Relocation Management Company was acquired by Merrill Lynch. One of the advantages of dealing with Merrill Lynch, Mr. Atwood feels, is the decision of higher management to allow a significant degree of autonomy in the operation of each subsidiary. He is therefore interested in buying a company in which top management wants to remain with the business for many years to come.

To understand the future impact of the national real estate companies, let us examine their potential attractiveness to buyers, sellers, salespeople, and third party purchase companies.

ATTRACTIVENESS TO BUYERS

People do business with people they know or think they know. All of us have "comfort zones" in selecting the actions we are going to take in any given decision making process. The greater recognition a company has, the more comfortable people feel in doing business with that firm.

A national company with an effective national institutional ad campaign can gain that needed recognition and nurture it over a period of time. A national can sell your home in Des Moines and find your new home in Orlando. They could advance the equity in your current home to facilitate the timely purchase of the new one.

During the listing of the current home and search for the new one, the buyer can be comfortable in the fact that the same company is involved in both transactions and therefore able to effect a smooth transition. With the type of training and career opportunities available to the sales staff, buyers will be attracted to the professional career minded sales team that services them in their house hunting needs.

National companies will also be able to help with

financing through ownership of mortgage lenders and/or large lines of credit for interim financing needs. Large national companies will have enough capital to fund their own home warranty programs. This obviously will be another drawing card for buyers' business.

Buyer loyalty has long been a notorious problem in the real estate brokerage business. If one broker could not find the right house, the buyer could go down the street to another broker for similar services. This will change with the maturation of national companies. Buyers will be more inclined to stick with a national company longer until the home is purchased. They will do this because the national sold their previous home, has a more secure image than most, plus, it has a vast array of services not available from small firms.

ATTRACTIVENESS TO SELLERS

All sellers want the same things. These are the highest price, in the shortest period of time, with the least inconvenience. National real estate companies will be able to do all three of those things better than anyone else! It is simply a matter of exposure. The greater exposure the property receives, the better the odds that the seller will receive the results desired.

What tools can a national utilize in the listing situation? A local and national sales force that is well trained, paid and motivated, huge institutional and product advertising budgets using every modern mass media and local media device under the direction of skilled professionals, a tight national referral program that delivers buyers from all over the country to the seller's front door, national contracts with third party purchase companies and corporations that give control of transferring executives solely to a certain national company.

Because of the "big is best" syndrome, sellers will feel that the biggest company will bring the best results. Look around your MLS. Do you see the big Realtors getting larger each year or smaller? Remember, also, that the current big Realtor in your town will not even approach the size or the diversity of services available from the nationals.

The growing situation of the haves and have nots in the real estate brokerage business will be made very clear to sellers in the listing presentation when a local broker is competing with a national company.

ATTRACTIVENESS TO SALESPEOPLE

Brokers always tell the new real estate applicant that they are looking for career minded salespeople. But what kind of career opportunity is available with today's broker? When a salesperson has proven himself in the field, where does he go from there? He usually goes out the door and opens a real estate company of his own or he jumps to another office that will offer some advantage either real or imagined. Stop and think about it! What career opportunities are there with your firm today or tomorrow? Maybe a branch managership or in a very few occasions some ownership or a percentage of profits.

We have never been very successful in attracting the college graduate into our business. Most people in this business tried their hand in another line of work before landing in real estate sales. This is beginning to change, but not on a large scale.

What will the national be able to offer the aspiring real estate professional? Listen to the following story.

Gary Graduate is interviewing on his college campus with recruiters from various corporations all over the country. One of the recruiters is from National Realty, Inc., a real estate company with 475 offices and 11,000 salespeople and administrative personnel throughout the U.S.

Gary is getting his college degree in Marketing with a minor in management. He wants to get his experience in direct sales and eventually work into management with a company that can give him upward mobility through the organization based on merit.

Neal, from National Realty, Inc., lays out the following career path for Gary. He will first become licensed through the company run pre-license school. Upon being licensed, Gary will attend the two month intensive sales course given at the main office in Atlanta. Upon graduation from the sales course, Gary will be assigned to a local office in his home town.

He will be in direct sales for two years, during which time he will receive periodic enhancement seminars to refine his selling skills. Also during this time, Gary will be given six month reviews by his immediate manager. If his progress is satisfactory, he will be given an assistant manager's position in a small office.

From then on, Gary's career up the corporate ladder depends on skills and determination. If he continues to do well, he could become a manager of a small office, then a medium size office, a large office, a whole city with numerous offices, and an entire region with responsibilities for the sales done in a certain state like Illinois or Ohio.

From these positions he could move into the corporate headquarters where he would take on a staff function with the mortgage division, warranty division, corporate relocation division, merger and acquisition division, public relations division, or one of many others. After a good working knowledge of the whole company from the corporate headquarters point of view, he could assume total responsibilities for the western states region comprising the efforts of 125 offices and 3,500 people working in 14 states. Does all this sound unbelievable to you? Far fatched? Unrealistic? Look at stories of Coldwell Banker and A. E. LePage and see what they have achieved thus far!

ATTRACTIVENESS
TO RELOCATION COMPANIES

Relocation companies (sometimes called third party purchase companies) are gaining an ever increasing foothold in the executive transferee area. Most corporations that retain the services of a relocation company have different divisions and offices located in numerous cities in the U.S. and internationally.

In order to service these national firms, the third party company must choose a Realtor to handle the listing of a transferee's home. Another Realtor must be chosen in the city to which the transferee is moving. More than likely both Realtors will not know one another and will not run their businesses in the same way. The listing broker will not be able to help the transferee by providing much information on the new real estate market that he is moving into. Also, the selling broker can't be informed on the kind of situation that his new customer is leaving behind in his previous home.

If the third party company worked exclusively with a national company that had offices in both cities, the transfer could be coordinated by the corporate relocation department of the national company. This makes the job of the third party company much easier. It also puts the total responsibility for the sale of the existing home and the successful purchase of the new home in the hands of one person. If there are problems with the sale or purchase, one person is accountable to the third party company. Third party companies like this. They want one person responsible for the total move.

Working with one or two national companies also simplifies the record keeping function of a third party company tremendously. Currently, files must be maintained on the preferred Realtors in each city. New ones must be added and others deleted. Statistics on the quality of services rendered by each broker must be kept and periodically reviewed.

When working with a national real estate company with a central corporate referral division, all the filing can be reduced to analyzing the performance of the national company as a whole. Instead of keeping in contact with 300 different Realtor firms across the country, just one contact is necessary with the national company. The policing of the quality of service is then the responsibility of the internal checks and balances designed by the national company to maintain standards.

SUMMARY

The real estate giants are certainly beginning to emerge. Their collective impact on the brokerage business will be awesome! Some analysts predict that 10 firms will control 80% of all the residential brokerage business done across the country.[15]

Although the exact percentage is conjecture at this point, it is fair to conclude that strong national brokerage firms will enjoy a large market penetration.

3 RELOCATION COMPANIES

How would you like to call on one man who is going to give a total of 9255 listings to Realtors in one year? As a matter of fact, he will control more listings next year and in many years yet to come. His name is Dr. Weston E. Edwards and he is chairman and chief operating officer of Merrill Lynch Relocation Management, Inc.

Yes, in calendar year 1977, Dr. Edwards (doctorate degree from Harvard Business School and previous faculty member) and his firm had some remarkable achievements:

—268 corporations using MLRM for transferee related services

—496 MLRM employees

—9,255 homes acquired from transferring employees of client corporations

—16,000 employees served

—$76,700,000 in annual gross revenues.
  According to George Rathman, of Merrill Lynch,

57

U.S. corporations spent over 3 billion dollars transferring 200,000 homeowners around the country in 1977."[16]

The cost of transferring an employee in America in 1977 was $16,000 on the average.

Because of the huge cost and increasing problems related to employee relocation, corporate employers are beginning to turn in increasing numbers to relocation specialists. In 1975, 36% of corporations surveyed used relocation companies to some degree. That figure went up in 1976 to 40% and 45% in 1977.

Just think of it! Forty-five percent of America's large corporate employees seeking the services of specialists who are outside the real estate brokerage field.

Of the $16,000 cost to move an employee, only $3,300 represented brokerage fees. The other costs included employee travel and temporary living, family travel and shipment of household goods, duplicate housing, loss on sale below fair market value, closing costs, equity advances, purchase and resettling in new home, and reimbursement for additional tax liability.

As you can see, there are many costs and complexities that arise when an employee agrees to a reassignment in another part of the country. As corporations seek professional help in this area, more relocation companies are formed and the competition for corporate clients becomes intense.

Let us forget our roles as real estate people for a moment and take a good look at the facts involved in the corporate transferee business.

Relocation companies are also referred to as 3rd party purchase companies. The employer is the first party, the employee is the 2nd party in a transfer and the relocation company steps in as the 3rd party in this triangle. The function of the 3rd party company working on behalf of the employer is to help the employee relocate in his new home as quickly and as worry free as possible. The corporation wants a minimum of cost to itself, a high degree of satisfaction to the employee, and a minimum of lost work time by the transferee.

Each year Merrill Lynch initiates a study of the relocation policies of the top 1,000 industrial companies in America as listed by *Fortune Magazine*.

STATISTICS

From 686 interviews conducted in the spring of 1978, the following facts were uncovered regarding calendar year 1977:

Companies with the largest numbers of transferees were in the following industries:

Business machines . . . 788 Transferees Annually
Rubber products . . . 321 Transferees Annually
Retail and wholesale . . 319 Transferees Annually
Petroleum and gas . . . 291 Transferees Annually[18]

Corporate policies on disposing of present home:

Employee Reimbursed for Selling Expenses   43%
Relocation Company Purchase Home 36%
Employer Purchase Home 12%
No Assistance or Reimbursement . . . . . . 8%[18]

Percent of companies reimbursing for following categories:

Brokerage Commission 81%
Cost of Living Differential 31%
Temporary Living at New Location . . . 98%
Househunting Trips 98%
Shipment of Household Goods 97%
Additional Allowance for Incidentals 75%
Reimbursement for Additional Income Tax
Liability Resulting from Payment of
Non-deductible Expenses 58%
Duplicate House Carrying Expenses 50%
Mortgage Discount Points 43%
Mortgage Prepayment Penalty 58%
Maintenance, Repair or Remodeling Costs . . 13%
Loss on Sale Below Fair Market Value . . . 26%
Loss on Sale Below Investment Costs 16%
Other Normal Closing Costs . . . . 75%[18]

HIGH COST OF MOVING AN EMPLOYEE

All of these statistics point to one major conclusion. *American industry has made the commitment to spend huge sums of money in order to entice employees to relocate into areas where they are needed most.*

Traditionally real estate people always valued their contacts in industry who would send employees directly to them when selling or buying. This pattern is beginning to change. Relocation companies have the financing and staff to provide help in all the categories listed above. Because the sale of the employee's current home and purchase of the new one must be handled by two brokers in different parts of the country, a relocation company can be effective in coordinating both ends of the deal.

Large sums of money can be provided by relocation companies to purchase homes of employees, thus freeing up the employer's capital funds. Many of the relocation companies sell their services to an employer on the basis that they can actually save dollars for the employer and provide more valuable benefits for the employee than the employer can do on his own!

Most relocation companies are paid a percentage of the price of the home they acquire or a reduced percentage figure with the employer paying all direct costs. Let's look at an example of each:

Example No. 1

Price paid for employee's home $50,000
Fee for relocation company (17%)   8,500
Brokerage commission and other related costs are paid to the relocation company out of the percentage figure.

Example No. 2

Price paid for employee's home $50,000
Fee for relocation company (2%)   1,000

Brokerage commission and other related costs are passed on to employer.

The single biggest impact made on this author in researching the material for this chapter is the high degree of professionalism displayed by relocation company personnel and the rather sophisticated and thorough process through which they render their services to today's transferee. To illustrate, let us review some thoughts proposed by Dr. Weston Edwards at a seminar held in 1978.

He states that American industry has made some major policy changes in reference to the transferee. These changes include a substantial increase in offering to buy the employee's home, more complete reimbursement of both home sale and home purchase expenses, more frequent reimbursement for the nondeductible items relating to moving, relocation benefits being extended to new hires as well as current employees, and longer offer periods in home buying plans.

All of these major policy changes were designed to ease and expedite the moving process for a valued employee.[16]

FEWER TRANSFEREES

Recent statistics have shown that the number of transferees in America is *declining* and not increasing as you would probably expect. The biggest reason that transfers are declining is the women's movement. The spouse is not as willing as she used to be to uproot her family and it is also possible that she may have a job of her own that she would be reluctant to leave.

Some relocation companies are beginning to provide the service of helping wives secure new employment in the area being moved to. In other households, the woman's job is the higher paying and/or more important than the man's, thus resulting in an obvious reluctance to move on her part.

A huge difference in home values between cities poses yet another reason for a decrease in the number of transferees. When moving to an area of substantially higher priced homes, the transferee must lower his standard of living by purchasing a home he can afford though not equal in size or quality to the home left behind.[16]

INCREASED RELUCTANCE TO TRANSFER

A subtle change is also beginning to permeate the corporate ranks. More and more people today show an increased preference for a higher quality of life and not necessarily higher pay. Corporations previously felt that its employees either moved up or out. Today they are more understanding of the employee who does not want to be moved for personal reasons. Because of the $16,000 cost to move an employee, many corporate employers are scrutinizing their transferee policy more closely and are becoming more cost conscious.

As the trend toward transferring diminishes somewhat, corporate employers are using relocation companies more and the actual benefits offered are on the rise.

It appears, then, that employers are encountering more resistance to the corporate transfer than in the past. In order to overcome the reluctance to move, more benefits are being offered to entice good people to relocate where they can do the company the most good.

More benefits are available today because companies want to remain competitive within their industry. As relocation policies become more liberalized, this fringe benefit takes on greater importance when designing a viable recruiting program.

The only reason that a transfer is made is, of course, to provide the transferee's talent and abilities to his new assignment. Toward this end, it is imperative that the move be made in an expeditious manner with a minimum of time consuming distractions. A relocation plan that is well conceived and professionally implemented assures a minimum of lost time on the job for the transferee.[16]

NEW CHALLENGES FACING EMPLOYERS

Although the potential for relocation companies is enormous, so are the challenges. The growth of the women's movement and the widening gap in property values will continue to be limiting factors on the number of qualified people willing to accept a corporate transfer. In regard to the women's movement and working wives, there have been some instances in which the wife was the one transferred because of the importance of her job.

Because home values are increasing at a rapid rate, another problem faces the employer today. Most transferees consider the purchase of a new home to be more an investment rather than a search for decent shelter. They want to maximize the profit on the home they are selling and do a lot of very cautious house hunting before making an offer on that new home. In fact many transferees are asking for longer periods in which to sell their present homes before taking the company offer. They also want an extended period for house hunting in the new city.

Both of these attempts to maximize the profitability of both real estate transactions actually works to the detriment of the employer. The more time spent in selling the present residence and searching for a new one, the longer it will take before this transferee will be able to contribute his or her talents to the new job assignment.[16]

NEW EMPLOYEE BENEFITS

Some benefits being suggested to make a transfer more appealing could include the following:

Job Finding Assistance for the Spouse
Many times the second job in the family is vital to

maintain the standard of living to which the married couple have become accustomed. It is therefore a good idea to consider giving aid to the spouse by providing information on job opportunities in his or her chosen field of endeavor.

Full Relocation Benefits to New Hires
In the case of college graduates, the cost of extending relocation benefits is less costly because many may be single and/or may not have accumulated many material goods that need moving. The first move for a new hire and its professional or unprofessional handling will probably make a lasting impression on the new employee. It could affect his or her willingness to accept more transfers in the future.

Mortgage and Equity Loan Financing
As the difference in home values continues to widen between various regions around the country, an increasing number of transferees will need financial assistance to complete the purchase of the new residence.

Cost of Living Differential
The disparity in prices of homes and other goods and services between different metropolitan areas has fostered an additional relocation problem. Should the employer render additional compensation to those employees who are moved into a higher cost area? Once accustomed to the higher income, will those transferees be willing to move to a lower cost area in the future with a lower income that has had the cost differentials? There is also a strenuous effort being made to label the additional compensation received as a temporary adjustment to income. The transferee should constantly be reminded that the cost differential that is paid will always vary when relocating from one locale to another. The need for cost differential compensation is becoming more necessary as living costs differ by as much as 30 to 40% in some areas.

Reversing the Transfer

This last suggestion seems costly and far fetched but may be necessary to entice some key people to uproot their family. Tell the employee that the company will move him and his family back to his former location if the family is unable to adjust to the move. This could be a powerful tool in persuading the spouse to consent to the transfer. Like anything, of course, this concept has its drawbacks. The spouse, children, and even the employee himself may not give the move a chance to work if they always have the option of returning to their previous home.

Also, will there be a position for the employee in the branch office or plant that he was transferred from? His position may have been taken by someone who is better qualified or the budget for that office cannot justify his salary in addition to the management team currently in place.

Evidently, the offer to move back is quite common in overseas moves. It would be an interesting concept to study in domestic moves.[16] The implementation of this policy would obviously be great for the relocation companies and real estate brokers.

At the beginning of this chapter, certain statistics were presented showing the volume of business done by Merrill Lynch Relocation Management Company in 1977. The 1978 figures are very revealing. The total income has jumped from $76,700,000 in 1977 to $109,500,000 in 1978. This is a percentage increase in total income of 43% in one year. The number of homes purchased in 1977 grew from 9,255 to 11,500 in 1978; an improvement of 22%. The number of employees actually served went from 16,000 to 21,000 which represents a growth of 31%. All of this growth took place with the addition of only 45 employees, giving a total staff size of 541. This would indicate an apparent increase in efficiency in serving an additional 5,000 transferees.

As was mentioned in the preceding chapter, the Coldwell Banker Company of California acquired a 50% position in Executrans, which is a relocation company in competition with Merrill Lynch, Home Equity and others.

The Coldwell Banker story is an example of a very large brokerage firm getting into the relocation business. The Merrill Lynch story is just the reverse. This is an example of a relocation company getting into the real estate brokerage business.

The new entity in Stamford, Connecticut, Merrill Lynch Realty Associates, will be forming a national real estate brokerage firm by acquiring existing brokerage companies across the U.S. As these companies are acquired, they will probably receive the listings on those homes purchased by the Merrill Lynch relocation company in their area.

It seems logical that the promise of giving all these controlled listings to an acquired brokerage firm is one of the incentives for accepting an offer to purchase each firm.

Besides Merrill Lynch, who are some of the other large relocation management companies? The acknowledged pioneer in the relocation field is Homequity, Inc. of Wilton, Connecticut. Homequity pioneered the home purchase concept in 1964. To show how the volume of homes purchased has grown, it took from 1964, to June 1973, for Homequity to buy its 20,000th home. That represents an average volume of only 2,000 a year. The number of homes bought in 1978 approximates 9,600.

Another concept begun by Homequity was the introduction of the Homerica program in 1955. The Homerica division deals not with the sale of the existing home, but the finding and purchase of the transferee's new home.

Today, certain Realtors have installed costly studios in their offices designed in accordance with specifications given by the Homerica division. These studios are for the purpose of receiving a transferee into your office in a professional environment. A visual program is presented to acquaint the newcomer with the local market.

Those brokers installing a Homerica studio also are the recipients of the Homequity listings in their area.

In 1971, Homequity was merged into a large national management services company entitled Peterson, Howell and Heather, Inc. The parent company provides a variety of management services for many corporations around the country.

The major service provided by the parent company is an extensive leasing program for cars, trucks, business aircraft, computers and other equipment. The merger benefitted Homequity by giving it a stronger financial base and an entree to the hundreds of companies already involved in leasing programs with the parent company.[11]

Executrans is another relocation company to watch for in the future. (Approximately 2,600 homes acquired in 1978.) Equally owned by Sears and Coldwell Banker, it will probably prove a good match for Homequity and Merrill Lynch. Its credentials begin with the backing of the nation's largest retailer and largest Realtor.

Equitable Relocation Corporation (approximately 5,000 homes purchased in 1978), owned by the Equitable Life Assurance Society and Relocation Realty Corp., owned by Control Data Corporation[12] also will continue to grow and be very competitive.

In each case, all companies mentioned in this chapter are owned by huge financially powerful corporations. These relocation companies have obviously been acquired in anticipation of large revenues.

DESIRABILITY OF TRANSFEREE BUSINESS

The transferee is the most preferred home buyer or seller for many reasons. Most transferees are in the middle to upper income range and have a minimum of trouble qualifying for their financing. They definitely will sell their present home and they will purchase a new home. There can be no doubt as to their motivation! They usually purchase homes in higher price ranges than average, thereby generating larger real estate commissions. They must sell and buy in a limited time frame, thus assuring a commission in a relatively short period of time. They are typically more experienced in home buying and more decisive in their likes and dislikes.

Because transferees spend only two or three years in a home in many instances, a good salesman is assured of a listing from a happy purchaser when they are transferred out of town. For these and other reasons, the transferee is a very desirable client to any Realtor.

THE CONCENTRATION OF POWER

The number of transferees available to the average Realtor is shrinking every year. In 1977, Merrill Lynch purchased 9,255 homes of transferees and gave the listings on those homes to Realtors of its choosing. In 1978, the number of controlled listings in the Merrill Lynch arsenal increased to 11,500.

Because of the increased number of homes acquired, 2,245 fewer listings were available to the normal competition between Realtors. They were actually pulled out of the marketplace and brought under Merrill Lynch's complete control. That's power!

You may react by saying that 11,500 listings are an insignificant number when compared to the national residential real estate volume sold each year. More important than the number, however, is the trend. Remember that in 1975, only 36% of America's corporations used relocation companies. That percentage grew to 40% in 1976, and 45% in 1977.[18]

The relocation business is booming! The future is very promising and the competitors are not that numerous.

Because of the number of homes purchased in a year by the typical relocation company, the demand for capital is sizeable. In 1978, Merrill Lynch purchased 11,500 homes.

Let us look at some hypothetical numbers:

Number of homes purchased 11,500
Hypothetical average price $70,000
Hypothetical average equity $30,000
Total equity advances to transferees
(11,500 x $30,000) $345,000,000
Number of days equity tied up until sale
and closing .... .120 days
Average capital tied up in 1978, at any
one time in purchased homes ... $115,000,000
Add equity advances and other commitments—
total cash outlay at one time 200 to 300 million
dollars.

This gives an indication of the enormous capital· that could be necessary to handle the volume of business outlined previously. Unlike the real estate brokerage business, the relocation business will be composed primarily of financial giants with vast lines of credit.

What does this kind of power in the hands of a few corporations mean to the average Realtor today? What will be the effects in the future? *The overwhelming impact is that the once independent Realtor is growing more dependent on forces outside his business for survival.* As the transferee market turns in larger numbers to relocation companies for help, the Realtor will have to persuade relocation companies that he can best serve their brokerage needs in his area.

CERTIFIED BROKER PROGRAM

On the other hand, those Realtors large enough to adequately service the needs of relocation companies in each market will enjoy a bonanza of steady business if a relocation company favors them with its patronage.

A new concept employed by Merrill Lynch could sweeten the pot even more for certain large Realtors. This concept is entitled the "certified broker program." Basically it calls for the selection of only one brokerage firm in each metropolitan area to service all Merrill Lynch transferees in its location. This assures dedication by the local Realtor to satisfy all referred customers. It also gives Merrill Lynch leverage with the certified brokers to guarantee good service. If the service is not satisfactory, all business could be yanked and given to another company.

A training program is required by Merrill Lynch for all managers in the brokerage firm. This is intended to bring a certain standardization to handling of transferees by all Realtors participating in the certification program.

IDEAL BROKER STRUCTURE

What are the criteria that a relocation company uses in evaluating a prospective broker? High on the list are a *proven track record* in the area, and *one capable person* in the broker organization who is accessible and in a decision making capacity.

One other factor is extremely important to the relocation companies. The servicing broker must give very close *attention to administrative detail*. With hundreds and even thousands of homes in inventory at any one time, the relocation company must have frequent and accurate reports on every property currently listed. These reports will give an up-to-date status of the property's physical condition, and necessary repairs or maintenance required to keep it sharp.

If work is required, the broker is expected to recommend a course of action to rectify the problem. He must retain the talent required, oversee the work, and forward the invoice for payment after approving it. Simply stated, the listing broker is a kind of property manager on each listing until the home is sold and closed.

Weekly or biweekly reports are also expected detailing current market conditions, number of showings on each home, copies of ads run in the local papers, and any other efforts put forth by the listing broker to sell the property. Because the relocation company is relying on the listing broker to accurately keep it informed, these reports must be truthful and candid.

A great salesman who is poor on detail and lazy in reporting to the relocation company will not have corporate listings long! They want good service and aggressive sales organizations but they also expect to be constantly updated on the status of each property.

In an article entitled "Courting The Third Party Company," Mr. William Tugeau, vice president of Homequity/ Homerica, mentions that the ideal broker organization to service a third party company is one in which there is a *designated relocation director.* This permits the entire brokerage firm to service the listings and buyers while enabling the channel of communication to and from the relocation company to be through one person. *The relocation company doesn't want to know every "hot shot" salesman in the brokerage company!*

The relocation director is given the leads and he or she is responsible for the satisfactory servicing of the transferee. Who actually does the job in the organization is of no interest to the relocation company. The director is the only line of communication and must get the results expected. In this arrangement, the above reports previously described would be sent first to the relocation director in the brokerage company and then forwarded to the relocation company. Many medium to large firms across the country now understand the needs of their corporate and relocation company clients and have installed a capable individual in the position of relocation director.

When placing listings in small metropolitan areas, the relocation director position is not feasible for most brokers due to inadequate transferee volume. In these instances the principal of the firm or someone in a decision making capacity is preferred. Regardless of the brokerage size, however, the proper and professional handling of the referred customer is expected.

The average relocation company is deluged with inquiries by brokers who are anxious to service relocation customers.[10]

If given the opportunity to work with a relocation company, be conscientious, be thorough, send in the reports when requested, and your relationship can be a very profitable one for a good long time. Remember, there are other brokers who want a crack at the corporate business too.

REAL
4 ESTATE
FRANCHISES

From statistics generated by the National Association of Realtors in September of 1978, the franchise impact on real estate brokerage is becoming apparent. Only 8.5% of those Realtors responding to a national survey were affiliated with a real estate franchise in 1975. Three years later, that percentage has doubled and now stands at 17%.[17]

An article in the September 4, 1978 issue of *Forbes Magazine* listed six major national franchisors. They included Gallery of Homes, Inc., with 758 offices in 49 states, Red Carpet Corporation of America, with 1,200 offices in 16 states, Century 21 with 6,039 offices in 48 states, Electronic Realty Associates, Inc., with 1,650 offices in 46 states, Realty World Corporation, with 1,147 offices in 36 states, and Better Homes and Gardens Real Estate Service, a newcomer with 500 offices.[7]

Other firms are in the real estate franchise business operating both nationally and regionally. The six listed above, currently (October, 1978), have a significantly larger number of member offices than any others.

Many Realtors have not gone the franchise route for numerous reasons. Some Realtors are enjoying success and feel that the costs of franchising outweigh the benefits. Other Realtors see the inroads being made by franchises in their markets and are confused about what to do. Still others would like many of the benefits of franchising, but have not found a franchise organization that appeals to them.

Because the whole concept of franchising real estate brokerage firms is only about 8 years old, new converts were slow at first. Many of the early franchisees latched onto a franchise to compensate for their poor competitive showing against the more successful firms in each market.

Many Realtors still feel that franchises are for marginal companies that need a helping hand in order to survive. National statistics do show that the average income of franchisees is below that of the independent Realtor.

It is true that many weak companies have been attracted to franchises. Some of these have become stronger and some have not survived. The success or failure has been on the part of the franchisee or the franchisor or both depending on particular circumstances.

THE SELECTIVE FRANCHISOR

As the franchising concept begins to mature, good stable companies are opting for membership in a franchise group. Some franchises employ a basic marketing philosophy of selectivity. The growth of these new franchise companies is necessarily much slower than the wildfire spread of the larger franchises. The good companies attracted to a selective franchise want to be affiliated with quality companies only. They also want geographic boundaries drawn to guarantee their exclusive use of an area for opening additional offices. The expanding choices available among franchises will give the Realtor more possible alternatives. In a healthy competitive atmosphere, franchises will be required to become more professional and offer more professional services. Do not, then, classify all franchises as appealing to marginal companies.

THREE IMPORTANT CRITERIA

As there are strong and weak Realtors, there are also strong and weak franchisors. Franchise companies can be classified as weak if they are too thin in *three* categories. *First,* they may be *undercapitalized for the market penetration they are attempting to service.* In other words, their income and/or original investment may be insufficient to enable them to financially afford to provide the services promised. *Secondly,* the *number of offices in a particular geographical area may be inadequate* to justify proper training facilities and instructors, a sizeable institutional advertising budget, or periodic consulting and co-ordination. *Third, the support staff of the franchisor may be ill-equipped to follow through on services promised* due to lack of ability and background in the real estate business, insufficient numbers of people, or inadequate leadership.

Some states have franchising laws which require a prospectus showing customers, ownership, income, profitability, and more. The prospectus must be given to each new franchisee before a franchise agreement is signed. If your state does not have such a law, be sure to obtain something similar from the franchise that you are considering.

THE SYNERGISTIC EFFECT

Franchising has proven in a dynamic way the overwhelming impact of the synergistic effect.

This concept dictates that the result of people working together toward a common goal will be much greater than the result of those same people working separately toward individual goals. Once in a franchise organization, you

75

benefit from your own efforts and the efforts of all other companies in your franchise. Every time a for sale sign goes up in front of a house, the public awareness of your common identity is increased.

Likewise, the insertion of an ad, the giving of a business card, mailing of direct mail literature, the wearing of a lapel pin, or any other act of promotion by any member of your franchise enhances its recognition in the mind of the general public. This synergistic effect on buyers and sellers creates the impression of bigness which brings with it a certain feeling of confidence and reliability.

Many franchises which possess little depth in staff personnel and programs have sustained themselves and their franchisees through the impact created by the synergistic effect. Do not sell it short. This phenomenon has far reaching repercussions on the attitudes and subsequent decisions of the buyers and sellers.

MAINTAINING LOCAL IDENTITY

The name and the logo of the franchise should be easily recognizable and easy to remember. For those considering a franchise, the question of local identity becomes important. Most companies that have been in business are hesitant to completely abandon their name. A franchise should allow for this by keeping the original name in conjunction with that of the franchisor. There has been some discussion in legislative bodies to establish a percentage rate for the size of each name. A popular theme would allow 60% for the franchise name and 40% for the local Realtor. The thinking is that the general public has the right to be able to easily differentiate between each franchisee by seeing the actual Realtor firm's name. It seems logical that combining both names on all signs, business cards, letterheads, and other advertising material, provides the recognition of the past and the large common image with which to build a strong future.

POWER OF PROFESSIONAL ADVERTISING

Probably more important than the name itself is the manner in which the franchise name is promoted to the public. Buyers and sellers will be impressed by the consistency with which it is displayed on television, for sale signs, newspaper ads, business cards, letterhead, office signs, brochures and other promotional media.

The professional touch of a good advertising agency can expand public recognition of a name and logo rapidly. Realtors pride themselves on the advantage of an old established name in their community. A sharp franchisor with a good ad agency can effectively use television to establish equal name recognition in a matter of a few months. The professional ad on television is proof enough for many people that those members of that franchise are also professional.

A recent research study found that 82% of all things that are learned are obtained by the sense of sight. It was also determined that 11% of all things learned are obtained by the sense of hearing. If these statistics have validity, it would appear that a medium that appeals to the senses of sight and hearing simultaneously would have enormous retention. In many instances, the franchises and their television blitzes have eroded the advantage enjoyed by the old established firms.

DENSITY OF OFFICES

One of the most often heard criticisms of franchises is over saturation of offices. There are instances of members of the same franchise next door to one another or across the street.

A certain degree of density is absolutely necessary for a number of reasons. Adequate training cannot be accomplished by a franchisor if there are too few offices in an area to fill the classes. Many people turn to franchises for

77

help in conducting a good, well structured training program primarily for the new licensee. If the offices are too sparse in a given area, there will not be enough franchise income from the local franchisees to finance a local training program.

Good density of offices is also important in the area of institutional advertising. A decent number of offices in a local TV market can all contribute sufficient funds collectively to finance a regular ongoing television campaign. The effect of synergism, mentioned earlier, is also increased dramatically as the density of franchised offices in a particular area intensifies. It would appear, however, particularly in a down market, that over saturation of offices can have a negative effect on some members.

The franchisee's inability to control the sales of the franchisor in his area would seem to be an additional matter for concern in the long run. What kind of equity is a franchisee building in his business if he has no exclusivity? What would a potential buyer be willing to pay for the business of a franchisee who has other competing companies with the same name in close proximity to him? The ideal franchise should allow for a decent amount of density and some provision for exclusivity on the part of each franchisee.

EXCLUSIVITY OF AREA

Exclusivity would seem to be an inherent quality of a franchise. If you were to buy a MacDonald's hamburger franchise, you would want a guarantee in writing that the franchisor would not sell another franchise too close to your store. If another MacDonald's was allowed too close to you, it would harm you in two ways. First it would take some of the customers away who would have purchased from you. Secondly, the value of your business to a potential purchaser would be diminished by the lack of a sufficiently large enough exclusive area. The exclusivity of an area refers to the restraints put on the franchisor.

In an exclusive area agreement the franchisor is promising in writing that no additional franchises will be sold to any other person in the geographic area agreed upon. This gives you the peace of mind that your efforts in an area will not be undermined by an unscrupulous franchisor who is looking only for numbers of offices regardless of the consequences.

When the day comes to sell your business, you are selling two things of value; your going business and the exclusive ownership of the franchise in your area. If someone wants to become a member of your franchise in your area, they must buy it from you.

The author was the beneficiary of this exclusivity when he sold his franchise in Earl Keim Realty. Even though he was leaving the business as the biggest producer in the office, the buyer had confidence that the business would continue to succeed because of the ongoing support of the franchisor. Many brokerages have lost their share of business when the man who made it all happen finally called it quits. Not so with a franchise that permits exclusivity of area. Be sure to ask about it.

Because of the threat of national real estate companies as described earlier, franchises will have to provide a depth of services that can effectively compete with those of the national firms. To date, franchising has enabled the smaller companies to compete with the larger companies in each city. They have done it almost entirely with training programs, television, common for sale signs, and common advertising. Some have offered warranty programs and referral services also.

TRAINING

In discussing franchises and their respective services, we must turn our attention to the training function. Most brokers consider training as one of the most obvious benefits that franchising can offer. The two major categories of training available are sales training and management training. Both prelicense and post license sales training is standard with most franchise companies.

Until now, the post license curriculum has consisted of classroom sessions given by a full time training director. Topics covered include how to list, presenting the offer, the purchase agreement, time management, financing techniques, building referrals, improving self image, the for sale by owner, and other basic concepts. These classroom sessions have brought a certain degree of formality to the real estate training process. This is good because it gives the newly licensed person the impression that he or she is truly entering a profession.

Sales training, however, must go further than the original basics classes. To establish the necessary loyalties between salesman and broker, some training must be accomplished in the office between manager and trainee. The classroom knowledge obtained is really no indicator of success or failure in this business.

The "in office" training should get the new person into the field immediately after licensure. Management should not give the new person time to sit around the office and develop the bad habits of the old timers. A preset plan of assignments given by the manager to the new person can give direction to an eager yet inexperienced salesman. The "go and do and then come back and tell me about it program" gets the new person out where the customers are. When the trainee returns to the office, a debriefing session should be scheduled with the manager.

These sessions can expand the ability and loyalty of the new person. They also may lay the groundwork for a solid relationship of mutual understanding between manager and trainee. The manager learns about the capabilities and drive of the trainee and the new person begins to share his first experiences in real estate sales and learn what is expected by management.

Ongoing seminars are a part of the typical franchise package. These should be offered to the better salespeople. Too often, managers spend needless time with marginal performers instead of those who are the lifeblood of the sales force! These seminars usually last a half day and concentrate on one topic. A typical topic could be time management.

A million dollar producer could probably sell 50% more if proper time management techniques were utilized. No salesman knows all there is to know about selling. These seminars are intended to help a well running car shift into passing gear.

Franchises are also beginning to address themselves to management training. Most owners of residential brokerages have had little if any formal management training.

Management seminars are becoming an increasingly important part of the franchise overall training program. Today's sales manager must have more ability than before to properly compete with the complex and many faceted challenges that confront him. Subjects covered include management by objectives, goal setting, budgeting, motivating of salespeople, recruiting, interviewing, conducting a sales meeting, and others. The management training classes being offered are only a hint of the skills that must be mastered by tomorrow's sales manager.

CORPORATE RELOCATION

The preceding chapter dealing with third party companies discussed the amount of transferee business controlled by them. A franchise must form a corporate relocation department. The function of this department would be to conduct an ongoing, consistent lobbying effort aimed at third party companies and corporations that handle the corporate move with their own staff.

You don't have either the time or the contacts to obtain this business on your own. They want to deal with someone who has all the services to make their transferring employee satisfied. Usually most leads are given to the larger firms in each market. As the national companies come on the scene, they will also be calling on these corporations for their transferee business.

The franchises should have knowledgeable full time professionals who are constantly penetrating the third party and corporate field on your behalf. They will give the overall story of the strength of the franchise as a whole. You and your company will then be sold as the local expert on the scene.

If you hear of a company moving twenty families out of your area, you should be able to depend on your franchisor to supply the experts to call on that corporation on your behalf. If the statistics are valid that 20-30% of all transferees are handled by third party companies, your franchisor must be prepared to bring some of that business home to you.

HOME WARRANTY SERVICE

A home warranty program is now provided by most franchises. Most of them buy the service from outside warranty companies. It would appear ideal if the warranty service was provided by the franchisor directly rather than through an outside company. The real success of a warranty program is customer satisfaction and the referrals that are the result of well handled service calls.

Outside warranty companies obviously want your customers satisfied so that you will continue to use them. But, a franchise company which operates a warranty program itself, would be particularly sensitive to problems that arise. Its franchise income as well as warranty income is contingent upon the number of transactions that you generate. The extra income derived from a warranty company could enable the franchisor to be more profitable and more capable to provide first rate services to you.

ETHICAL STANDARDS

In another area, the franchisor must be responsible enough to monitor the business conduct of its members. Such a control device could be a periodic audit of the escrow accounts of each member. This could spot infractions of state license law and provide help to those who do not have a good system for handling the escrow account. Any deliberate violation of the license law could be grounds for dismissal from the franchise. This would provide assurance for all members in the franchise that a certain standard is being maintained.

MLS systems have arbitration committees, whose function is to settle disputes between members. Once settled, the parties agree not to continue to pursue the disagreement in the courts.

A franchise should also have a mechanism in place to prevent differences between franchisees from being exposed to the public. These committees made up of fellow franchisees, should also have a representative of the franchisor in attendance. Quick and fair settlement of a dispute by one's peers encourages harmony and good morale in a franchise organization.

NATIONAL REFERRALS

Another attribute necessary in a full service franchise is a good national referral service. The network must be widespread and represented by capable firms. Important also is the proper management of the referral network and a fair fee structure. The ability to provide service to the incoming or outgoing transferee is becoming more important. This importance will increase as national real estate companies begin to provide nationwide service through their network of offices.

ACCESSABILITY OF FRANCHISOR

The next criterion of a first rate franchise is accessability of the franchisor staff. The franchisor must be available to you to assure that all the above concepts are initiated properly in your company. Good programs without proper follow through will yield ineffective results. This accessability of the franchisor is important throughout your relationship but most necessary at time of conversion to the new franchisee identity.

In their eagerness to add new offices, some franchisors have sold faster than their ability to provide good follow through. Frankly, this is often one of the biggest complaints. Verify the past record of any franchise you may be considering. If satisfied, be sure that your franchisor spells out a calendar of events in writing. This written commitment should facilitate a smooth transition for you and your staff. It will also set the stage for a healthy franchisee-franchisor relationship.

ORIENTATION PROGRAM

Your staff of salespeople must have confidence in the decision you made to affiliate with a franchise. They will gain that needed confidence only if they fully understand the new services that they can now offer their clients. An initial orientation program should be conducted by the franchisor for your entire staff away from the office so that there are no distractions. A review one month later after they have had some experience would also be very beneficial.

CONSULTING

You as a manager and owner should be able to receive help from time to time on particular problems that arise. Most real estate managers have the same kinds of problems with recruiting, training, motivating, handling different personalities, advertising, escrow and general accounting functions, site selection, office layout, reimbursement, budgeting, office policy, and other areas. Because your franchisor works intimately with numerous Realtors, he should be able to inform and advise you on these matters.

BRAIN STORMING

Your local group of franchisees should be encouraged to meet periodically to discuss common problems and strategies. Your franchisor should be available to provide input for such meetings. One idea that resulted from one such meeting involved informing neighboring franchised offices of the existence of a new listing.

It was decided that each office would install a copying machine that transmitted over telephone lines. The monthly rental for this machine was $20.00. When a new listing was obtained in a certain area, all surrounding offices were sent a copy of the new listing immediately over the phone on the same day of the listing. With this copy, each office had a jump on their competition in being able to show it to their clients first. It also prevented the embarrassment of receiving a sign call on a new listing that the surrounding offices would have known nothing about.

CREDIBILITY OF FRANCHISOR

Before committing yourself to a particular franchise, one additional precaution may be warranted. Ask for a list of existing franchisees in your general area. Two questions should be asked each broker from the list given to you.

85

What is the quality of brokerage firms now in the franchise and how selective is the franchisor? Does the franchisor follow through on the promises made or implied at the time of signing the franchise agreement?

IMPACT OF FRANCHISING

Real estate franchising has dramatically altered the course of the residential brokerage business. Standardization has been proven a success in a previously conceived individualistic business. Television has been introduced into the marketing of real estate in many imaginative ways. Bigness has been sold to the public as being synonymous with such terms as professional, reliable, successful, and capable.

One of the most obvious contributions of franchising is the formalization of the training process for both sales and management personnel. Many Realtors now believe that brokers working together with a common identity, backed up by new expertise and services, can achieve greater heights of accomplishment than going it alone.

Before franchising, all Realtors had MLS membership and other services on an equal basis. Now the marketplace is topsy-turvy with some Realtors having huge competitive advantages over others. Franchising has been responsible for this imbalance.

As national real estate companies begin to penetrate each market, this imbalance will become more pronounced. *The environment in which you built your business will never be the same again!* Rapid innovation and the growth of franchises and national real estate companies will be commonplace.

Eventually, more capable people will be attracted into the residential brokerage field in unheard of numbers. As the trend toward bigness continues, more career opportunities will open up. College recruiting will be stepped up to attract the young career-minded person into the real estate business. The secrurity conscious young person will probably be drawn into the national companies, while the entrepreneur will go the franchise route.

You as a professional Realtor may feel that certain members of franchises are of poor quality and rather unprofessional by your standards. You may be right! The average homeowner sitting in his living room watching the television has his own thoughts. He doesn't see your ads on TV. He doesn't see large newspaper ads and branch offices all over town with your name on them.

By comparison, then, today's homeowner is impressed by professional TV ads prepared by first rate advertising agencies. The power of repetitive use of the mass media is having its desired effect.

If you own a medium size or relatively small company, you feel the daily frustration of recruiting and retaining good people in competition with strong franchise organizations. Why should a new person entering the real estate business come with your company instead of a franchise? What initial and ongoing training program do you have to offer? What kind of listing story can your salesman give in competition with a franchise? What are the current and future career opportunities in your company? The inroads made by franchising in most markets have made it necessary for you to ask some of these questions of yourself.

If the growth of franchises has tended to upset or confuse you, the growth of regional and national real estate companies will upset you even more! You are free to join a franchise of your choosing provided that the desirable franchises have not met their quota of offices in your area. The national real estate companies, on the other hand, will give you no such choice.

As more national companies come on the scene, I believe many more Realtors will view the real estate franchise as friend and not foe. In fact, the franchise may be your only viable hope to compete effectively with the national companies. The trends seem to indicate a real estate market that will be comprised primarily of national real estate companies, strong franchise organizations, and fewer independent Realtors. What direction are you going in? Think about it. Ask questions and investigate.

IMPLEMENTATION

In the foregoing discussion on franchising, many facets were covered. If, after investigation, you decide to join a franchise, use it completely. Understand all the programs offered and implement them. Most franchisees who failed never really took advantage of the services available.

Send your people to the training sessions recommended for them. Use the promotional literature, office decor ideas, signs, ad layouts and everything else that is offered. Most programs conceived by knowledgeable franchisors are the result of much experimentation. They won't work for you unless you use them.

Joining a franchise often permits the right occasion to make other improvements that you have been contemplating. Do them all at once and make things happen. Your enthusiasm and commitment will go a long way toward guaranteed success as a new franchisee.

COMPUTER
5 SERVICE
COMPANIES

In 1966, the average real estate salesman had a shoe box filled with MLS cards. These picture cards represented all the homes for sale in each geographic area. Another shoe box was filled with past sales, which was used for appraisal purposes. Some sales people kept these cards in loose-leaf style books. Still others kept them in little metal containers. Part of every working day was spent "doing my cards."

A master file was usually maintained by the office secretary to assure at least one up-to-date file of currents and comparables in the office. The duplication in record keeping throughout an entire multi-list system was incredible.

As an IBM salesman in Detroit, the author became fascinated with this incredible record keeping nightmare. At that time, Mr. Jack Jominy was the executive officer of the Western Wayne Oakland Board of Realtors in suburban Detroit. The author proposed the idea of centralizing the current and comparable files on one computer accessible by telephone. The inquiring salesman would tell the computer what kinds of properties were needed for a specific client. This was done by the use of a touch tone telephone. The computer had a recorded voice which would be given the right things to say and the inquiring salesman would write down the information given by the computer voice.

Mr. Jominy saw the obvious potential of the concept and began a crusade to bring this new tool into every real estate office in America. Twelve years later the crusade continues. As the pioneer in this field, he has watched the real estate computer industry grow and prosper.

This company, called Realtron Corporation, received additional entrepeneurial help and an infusion of needed capital when it was acquired by Mr. Hazard Reeves of New York City. Mr. Reeves was the guiding force and sole owner of Cinerama. With the successful launching of "Windjammer" and other films using the spectacular cineramic effects, Mr. Reeves realized millions for his genius and dogged determination.

Today, Realtron and other computer companies are offering a wide range of services to brokers across America. Although still a relatively new industry, the real estate computer companies are grossing millions of dollars of income annually from various services.

There are two basic categories of services now available from these companies. These are printing publications and online computer programs.

COMPUTERS IN MULTIPLE LISTING

The overwhelming majority of both printing and computer services are provided in co-operation with a multiple listing service. Current books are printed weekly displaying photos of all properties currently listed by all members of each multiple listing system. New listings are added each week while expired and cancelled listings are deleted. Any price changes or other important notations are also made to the file of properties before the book is printed.

The number of books used in each company will vary with the policy invoked by each broker. Some make it mandatory for each salesperson to have a personal copy. Others order only one or two for the entire office. Still others order one for the office and some salespeople order their own copies as they choose.

Comparable or sold books are printed periodically. These publications also include photos and detailed information on those properties that have sold since the last book was published. These books are used in the preparation of the appraisal of a property using the market approach. They can also be useful in persuading a potential buyer to make a reasonable offer on a piece of property. Once informed on prices recently paid for similar property, the buyer can draw a realistic offer based on factual and timely market data.

The current and comparable books briefly described herein are widely used across the country and enable today's sales professional to keep up-to-date with the market while having more time away from the record keeping chores to spend with buyers and sellers.

Originally, most multiple listing services printed separate sheets on each property and distributed cop es of these to the member offices so the salespeople could keep their shoe box files described earlier. As the size and sales volume of multiple listing services began to expand, the rapid dissemination of information to the member companies slowed considerably. It would not be unusual for a new listing to take two or three weeks to be processed by the MLS before it would be in all offices.

The tight listing situation experienced in the years of 1977 and 1978 spurred the use of computer services nationally. In fact, the ma'or computer companies grew in meteoric fashion in those two years. One of the most popular programs of computer services was the new listing information that could be received by member companies the same day it was received in the central MLS office. Each morning, a member broker could call the computer on the telephone and receive a complete printed list of all new listings sent to the MLS service the previous night. This list would be printed on a teletype machine located in the member's real estate office.

This rapid access to information on fellow broker's listings has obviously increased the odds of a property being sold by a co-operating broker rather than by an "in house" salesperson. In other words, the impact of computerizing current listing information, accessible by any member from a telephone, has enabled the MLS concept to operate at its maximum.

LARGE BROKER SERVICE

In addition to servicing members of a multiple listing service, today's computer companies also provide specially designed programs for some of the larger Realtor firms. Large multi-branch brokerage companies often have problems in getting the information out to all sales personnel in each office. A central file of all properties listed in a large brokerage firm is put on a separate file accessible only by those people who work in a particular company. This allows all salespeople in the organization to know about all listings in the company regardless of which branch has the listing. It also enables associates to show more properties listed within the company. This normally gives them the opportunity to earn a slightly higher commission on an in house listing.

As a further step, some large brokers have current and sold books printed by the computer companies showing only those properties listed and sold within the company.

INVESTMENT ANALYSIS

Other services provided include the computation ability of the computer used in analyzing investment property for a potential buyer. A five or ten year projection can be figured in less than a minute and typed out on a teletype machine. This projection could detail the expected performance of the proposed property for a particular investor and his tax bracket.

The planned acquisition of a single family home can also be analyzed to determine the tax advantages for a particular buyer. Anticipated inflation in value and loan amortization can be calculated to show the increased equity position realized by the proposed purchaser for five, ten, or even twenty years into the future.

THE GIANT FIRMS

The current leaders now in the real estate computer field are Realtron Corporation with corporate offices in Detroit and printing divisions in Detroit, Boston, and Pompano Beach, Florida. Besides being the pioneer in the industry, it is now the last privately held major real estate computer company in business.

Other leaders include International Graphics Corporation of Minneapolis. This company once privately held was acquired by the giant Moore Business Forms Corporation.

Multi-List Inc., of Denver, also a competing firm, was acquired by the well-known publishing firm, McGraw Hill, Inc.

Realtronics, Inc., is now owned by the very large and diversified Planning Research Corporation of McLean, Virginia.

The R. L. White Company of Louisville, Kentucky, was the recent acquisition of The American Broadcasting Company (ABC).

As in the other facets of the real estate business previously mentioned, the large corporations are now firmly entrenched in the real estate computer service field.

93

ONE CENTRAL COMPUTER
VS. MANY COMPUTERS

Although these computer companies do offer many similar services, their basic concepts of computerization do differ. Some of the companies install small computers in each city they service. Others have one large computer center accessible by toll free WATS lines from anywhere in the country. Depending on which company you are talking to, they will obviously justify their approach in the controversy of one large versus many regional small computers.

The national real estate companies being formed by Coldwell-Banker and Merrill Lynch will have need of computerization for effective communication between their many far-flung offices. One can see a branch office in Seattle sending a message by teletype about a transferee moving to the Chicago area. Daily listing and sales reporting, closings in process, cash flow requirements, and other timely information can be coordinated on a national basis.

Although computers will be a valuable tool to national real estate companies, they also play an interesting role when used in conjunction with MLS systems. Because computer service is available to any member on an equal basis, there tends to be an equalizing effect between the large and small broker. Both have the same information at the same time.

DEPENDENCY ON MANY CUSTOMERS

In fact, the very existence of the computer companies seems entirely dependent on a real estate industry comprised of many brokerage offices both large and small. This dependency on large numbers of individual brokerages appears to counteract other trends mentioned in this book. Large corporations such as Merrill Lynch are betting on the fact that its percentage of the real estate brokerage business will be substantial. Therefore the active acquisition of real estate companies is under way. If the market penetration of the large national firms does continue to escalate, many smaller companies may be forced out because they cannot compete.

The warranty companies are offering their services primarily to the large broker and those members of franchises, thus perpetuating the have and have not situation.

Then along come the computer companies, owned by corporate giants also, but dedicated to extending service to all firms regardless of size. It appears, then, that multiple listing, and the computer companies servicing them, are two of the prime forces striving for the continued existence of all brokerage firms large and small.

One thing is certain. The MLS systems and the computer companies are very dependent on a real estate market consisting of many different brokerage firms healthy and strong.

INCREASED USAGE

The exact role to be played by these computer companies in the future is only a matter of conjecture at this time. As the need for information intensifies and the pace of the real estate business quickens, the importance of computers will continue to escalate.

Let us look at computers from a different aspect for a moment. The National Association of Realtors in its profile analysis of its membership published in 1978 pointed out some interesting facts.

The average broker has been in the real estate business eleven years. Approximately half of all salespersons licensed today have been in the business less than three years.[17] This would seem to indicate that most brokers started their careers in the business without the help of computers as a practical tool. Conversely, half of the sales associates have been in the business during the greatest growth period of computerization in the brokerage business. Many sales associates use and believe in the advantages of the computer more than the brokers do. For this reason, many brokers still do not use a computer in their business because they got along without it and they think their salespeople can also. The average age of the broker in America is 49 years. The average salesperson is 42 years old.[17] This average is dropping as more young people begin to look on real estate sales as a profession. Obviously, the younger the broker becomes the more inclined he or she will be to utilize the computer in the daily operation of business.

HOME ANALYSIS

Another of the computer's advantages is the ability to perform rapid and complex calculations. Buyers are analyzing a potential home purchase as an investment and not just a place to raise their family. Computer programs are now available to show a prospective buyer how a certain property can perform from the investment angle.

The salesman types in to a teletype certain criteria including the buyer's tax bracket, down payment, financing available, inflation rate in that area, annual property taxes, and purchase price. In seconds, the computer begins printing out a report showing the return on investment for the next five or more years.

Items included in the report are *increase in equity* as a result of inflation in value and reduction in the mortgage balance, *total tax deductible dollars* to be subtracted from gross income annually, and *actual tax dollars saved* as a result of home ownership.

As the last twelve years have brought new uses for the computer in the real estate business, so the next few years will probably bring more. One concept talked about and hoped for would be the instant retrieval and transmission of a photo of each property desired. This would probably be the greatest breakthrough yet in the evolving progress of computerization. It may never happen and yet it may be announced tomorrow. We have talked about some of the history of computers in real estate and about possible roles in the future. Let's summarize by discussing the overall impact on today's Realtor.

IMPACT ON TODAY'S REALTOR

Computers have been a very positive force in helping sales associates and brokers perform many tasks. Computer services have become the backbone of the bigger and more advanced MLS systems around the country. Salespeople have had more free time away from needless record keeping to spend with buyers and sellers.

The general public has been better served by those Realtors using computers. Sellers have had information on their homes made available to all members of the MLS system quicker and in a more accurate form. Buyers have been able to rapidly eliminate properties that did not appeal to their needs. Buyers were also made aware of new listings quicker.

Computer services are and have been tied to the MLS system in each market. The computer usually cannot be offered to individual brokers until the local MLS system agrees to endorse one company over another. Once a particular company has been chosen, permission is given to store all information about current listings and past sales on the computer. Individual offices are then solicited by the sales staff of the computer company to purchase weekly photo books and or online computer service using a voice answer or printing teletype machine.

The equal access to these services helps to perpetuate the ability of all firms to compete effectively. In order to compete, each firm must have access to the entire inventory of current listings and past sales.

Unlike other sales businesses, the real estate sales person never really knows what he has to sell at any given moment. His product line is in a constant state of change.

This afternoon, the house at 123 Oak Street just went on the market at $56,900. Another home at 534 Willow, which had been on the market for two months, just sold one hour ago for $52,000. The house at 375 Main, which would have been ideal for a certain customer, was just taken off the market for personal reasons at 8:00 p.m. last evening.

The accurate recording of these changing vital facts is ideally suited to the capabilities of a computer. Regardless of any future realignment of the real estate industry, these examples will always be commonplace. The continued and even expanded usage of computerization in the real estate business seems guaranteed.

Investigate the possible uses of computerization in your business. No firm is too large or too small to benefit from this great tool.

HOME
6 WARRANTY
SERVICES

A young couple bought a home in Dearborn, Michigan, through the services of Earl Keim Realty in June of 1976. Included in the listed price was a warranty that covered certain items in the home for the first twelve months after the closing of the sale. One week after moving in, they received a home warranty contract in the mail from Guardian Home Warranty Corporation, an Earl Keim subsidiary. The contract listed the central air and heating systems, electrical and plumbing systems, hot water heater, dish washer and disposal as the major categories of items covered.

The seller, at time of closing, had paid $225 for the warranty program. The sale of this warranty marked a first for both Guardian and the home purchasers. It was the first warranty ever sold by this new company and it was the first time the couple had purchased a previously owned home that included a warranty program.

The association with the couple did not end with this one coincidence. In September of that year the 25 year old furnace in their home failed. The heat exchanger was found to be defective and the original manufacturer of the furnace had gone out of business years before. Because no replacements were being supplied by anyone, a new furnace had to be installed. Guardian wrote a check to the homeowners for $675, which covered the installation costs.

At the closing, the seller and the Realtor stepped out of an active relationship with the purchasers because their functions were completed. That was when Guardian stepped in to provide an ongoing service for the first twelve months of ownership. Although the seller's and Realtor's job was through, Guardian's was just beginning.

The home warranty industry is on the move! Through one growing pain after another, this new industry is beginning to mature. Some early entrepreneurs have failed and still others have survived and prospered. Is the warranty idea a temporary sales gimmick? Should your company sell such a program to your clients?

Here are some facts. According to an article in *Business Week,* 70,000 warranty policies were in effect nationally. Eighty percent of these had been purchased by the seller to be used as a sales tool. Electronic Realty Associates, Inc. (ERA), claims that its warranted homes sell in half the time at a 3% higher price than those homes not covered by a Warranty. Two large firms now expanding their efforts in the warranty business are St. Paul Fire and Marine Insurance Co. and The Title Insurance Company of California, the nation's largest title insurer. The 70,000 warranties now in effect represent only 2% of the 3.5 million used homes sold in the same period.[9] The potential for this growing industry is enormous!

COVERAGE

Let's look at the ingredients necessary to make an effective warranty program. What is the coverage inherent in the service? Most warranties available cover the heating and cooling systems, electrical and plumbing systems, hot water heater, and kitchen appliances. There are also some companies that have extended coverage on wells and septic systems, roofs, foundations, walls, ceilings, floors and other items not covered by the traditional homeowners policy.

The home warranty actually fills the gap left between homeowners coverage and those things the home buyer must repair at his own expense. Some of the above listed items such as roofs do have dollar limits of liability. An example would be $200 maximum for any damage to roofs not covered in the homeowners policy. Under each of the major categories, there are exceptions where no coverage is provided.

No repairs are paid by a warranty company when an item has been installed in violation of some FHA, VA, or city building code. Usually no coverage is included for anything outside the perimeters of the dwelling itself. The coverage is basically intended to apply to "wear and tear" situations.

A deductible dollar amount is specified in the contract to minimize what is referred to as nuisance claims. The normal deductible amount is around $50 per occurrence. Some are $100. The owners of the home are given instructions regarding service procedures when a problem arises. A phone call to a service number will put them in touch with the warranty servicing department. After verifying coverage, a serviceman will be dispatched to investigate the problem. The serviceman then calls the warranty company from the customers home to explain his findings. He then is given authorization to make the necessary repairs. The homeowner pays the deductible amount and the balance is billed directly to the warranty company. Some warranty companies require that work must be performed by certain contractors on an approved list while others have no such requirement.

WHO IS COVERED?

Most programs cover only the buyer beginning on the closing date and extending forward twelve months. The warranty fee is paid at closing by either buyer or seller. Sometimes the fee is split between both parties. A few companies give coverage to the seller as well as the buyer. This coverage commences 15 days after the listing and continues until the listing expires or the closing date if it becomes a pending sale.

This apporach provides a bonus to the seller for buying the program. It also has the element of being results oriented. No fee is paid unless the house sells and the closing is consummated. If an item goes into disrepair during the listing period, only the deductible is paid by the seller. The balance is taken care of by the warranty company. This means that some dollars are spent by the warranty company before any fees are received. In fact, some homes are improved by warranty work for the seller and no fee is ever paid to the warranty company. If the listing expires and there is no pending sale or renewal, the warranty company takes on some exposure without reimbursement. The seller coverage goes to the closing date; the fee is paid at closing and the buyer coverage begins.

Most warranties are now written to allow a Realtor to sell his warranty program to his buyer for coverage on anyone's listing. This is intended to get a little buyer loyalty while the house search is on. The buyer is told that warranties are now available on previously owned homes. He is also told that some listings on the market already have a warranty provided by the seller, but most listings do not.

Your company, which has a warranty service, will offer to sell him a warranty on any listing shown to him whether listed with your company or not. Why should he work with another company, then, if you can guarantee that he won't have to buy a home without some warranty coverage? Some purchase agreements are being written with a contingency clause that the warranty fee will be paid for by the seller or split between buyer and seller equally.

Companies differ on many of the specific terms of the contracts. As an example, assignability is allowed on some programs from one homeowner to another within the twelve month period. Others say that coverage ceases when the party covered sells the home. Some allow renewal for another twelve month term, while most terminate after the original year.

GROWING PAINS

Before leaving the discussion about coverage and the deductible amount, please keep one thing in mind. This is a whole new industry! Adequate actuarial tables have not been compiled to exactly determine how fees and coverages should be structured. Today, some fees are too high in proportion to coverage rendered, while the balance is tipped in the reverse direction with other firms.

Someone challenged the owner of the New York Yankees, George Steinbrenner, about the fact that the world series was not really a world series because only American teams were involved. He said that there was probably some truth in that but they did beat everyone that showed up!

Think of the home warranty services in the same way. They may not have designed the ideal coverage with the perfect fees and deductible amounts yet, but today's warranties are a lot better than the coverage our buyers ever had before.

SERVICE POLICY

A very crucial fact to determine is the particular service policy of the warranty company you may be considering. Are they fair? Do they value your patronage and extend themselves to satisfy your new homeowner? Do they sometimes show leniency on gray areas regarding coverage? Do they keep you informed on problems that have arisen and the outcome?

A well designed and administered service policy can bring many fine referrals into your brokerage firm long after the commission dollars have been spent. Poor follow up by the warranty company can have just the reverse effect. The only way to verify the quality of the service organization of a particular warranty company is to talk to existing Realtors who use their service. Take time to investigate. It can provide valuable insights for your final decision.

IMPLEMENTATION

Any warranty program that will be implemented on a wide scale must be easy for the salespeople to use. The paper work should be minimal and very straight forward in design. Your salesperson should have no burden of prior inspection or verification of condition of items covered.

Three elements are important for your salespeople to present the warranty to their customers. They must have adequate training on the approach to be taken in presenting the total program. Good visual aids should be made available by the warranty company so that the time and effort expended by the salespeople is cut to a minimum. Thirdly, you must ask that a form be signed by both buyers and sellers showing that the program was explained and they elected to take the warranty or declined.

Getting a buyer to sign is very crucial for your protection! If a buyer chooses to purchase a warranty for himself, he will obviously be covered. If, however, he chooses not to take it, you can minimize your involvement in future problems by keeping a signed copy of his refusal to participate in the program.

You want each buyer to sign on each deal for another reason. There have been instances where a buyer or his attorney has come back to the broker who offers a warranty program looking for help with a problem alleging that he was not offered the program. Once you begin to offer a warranty, be sure to cover yourself by demanding that all buyers sign a form at closing accepting or declining coverage.

What has accounted for the increased use of warranty programs around the country? The reasons are actually quite numerous.

ADDITIONAL SALES TOOLS

Sellers are the most common users of the warranties sold thus far. They see it as an additional merchandising tool to sell their house. The warranty companies are beginning to develop some clever sales aids to entice the seller into paying for the program. A sticker or sign rider is attached to the yard saying "warranted" or "one year protection" or something similar. Colorful brochures are left with the seller to be given each buyer who comes through the house. These brochures tell the buyer that this house has a one year warranty on the major working elements. It also goes on to explain how the program works and the many advantages to the buyer if he buys this home.

Tags or stickers are attached to all items covered so that people walking through the house can see all the coverage that has been provided by the seller. These sales aids are selling the buyer and giving him another reason to consider this home during the entire listing period. Institutional advertising in the form of radio and television spots are professionally prepared by the warranty company and made available to those brokers offering their warranty in each market.

PEACE OF MIND

Most sellers know that their home is not perfect and

things could break down in the first year of ownership. They can provide a warranty for their home buyer with the peace of mind that they have given the buyer someone to turn to after they take occupancy. Just as the seller turns the house over to its new owner, the warranty company takes over on the sellers' behalf to provide ongoing coverage for the next twelve months.

BUYER BEWARE

Another reason warranty sales are increasing is because the buyer now has someone to turn to after the sale. Purchase agreements have always used the words "as is," in referring to the condition of the house. This little clause has been intended to protect the seller and the Realtor. Theoretically, the buyer is relinquishing his rights to complain about subsequent problems because he is signing a document acknowledging that he is buying the property in an "as is condition." It is really a "buyer beware" or "caveat emptor" statement.

Doesn't it seem strange to you that warranties are available on almost everything we buy today except a used home? A home is the single largest investment most people make in their lifetime, yet they have no one to turn to when something goes wrong in the first year of ownership.

Warranties are available on new homes for a period of ten years. Now remember that these are brand new homes which have never been lived in or abused by a previous owner. Yet, until recently, we would ask people to invest in a dwelling that is perhaps 40 years old, that has had maybe 7 or 8 previous owners, without any kind of warranty or assurances that the working parts are reliable. It doesn't make sense! How has this practice gone on for so long without a warranty program of some kind?

Aside from helping buyer and seller, warranty programs are enabling Realtors to provide more services to their customers and gain more protection from subsequent problems after the sale. Every salesman who has ever sold any quantity of homes knows that the call from an unhappy buyer is the worst kind. The closing is over. The seller is gone. No money has been withheld in a contingency fund for subsequent problems with the house. Who is left to take the buyer's wrath? Your friendly Realtor.

Sometimes the Realtor is successful in getting help from the seller if the defect was known and the seller is willing to help. On other occasions, the buyer can be persuaded that he bought the home "as is" and it is now his problem. Still again, there are those times when the Realtor ends up contributing some dollars to keep the buyer happy in the hopes that he will relist his house when the time comes or he will give some referrals for the extra effort. Now the warranty program eliminates all that by giving the Realtor someone to handle the buyer problems.

CONSUMERISM

Other forces are at work to guaranty the future of the warranty concept. Consumerism has invaded every aspect of our free enterprise system. No product or service can be sold today without considering the health and well being of the consumer. "Buyer beware" is an idea whose time has long since past. The term that would probably be more accurate today is "broker beware."

Consumers expect the seller of a good or service to back it up with some kind of assurance for a specified time. You expect it on many other things you purchase. Why shouldn't your customers get it also?

In a November, 1978, recommendation made by the Federal Trade Commission (FTC), used car dealers were the subject. The FTC felt that used car dealers should be required to list the things that were defective with every car sold. Because the average buyer does not have a working knowledge of the intricacies of an automobile, the dealer should provide the expertise to point out flaws. As absurd as this may seem, this story is indicative of the impact of consumerism on today's businessman.

It also shows the growing involvement of federal and state governing agencies in the marketplace. Instead of requiring the original owners of those used cars to list problems, it was recommended to protect the consumer by applying pressure on the dealer. There are now some bills before state legislative bodies suggesting that the seller must guaranty the used house to the buyer for a certain period after closing.

The old "as is" clause is under attack. This will obviously lead to increased usage of warranty programs to protect the seller from future liability. It does not seem premature to say that all previously owned homes will carry a warranty program of some kind in the near future.

VIEWPOINT OF LENDERS

Lenders are becoming interested in the warranty programs. Many loan delinquencies are the result of high repair costs in the first year of ownership that jeopardize the consistent monthly payment of mortgage notes. This is particularly true with those buyers who use federally insured loans. The cost of replacing a hot water heater or repairing a furnace could be large enough to upset the mortgage payment cycle and begin the eventual delinquency and home abandonment.

Lenders now require title insurance and a home owner policy on each closing of an improved property. It now seems inevitable that home warranty programs will be mandated in the near future.

HOME OWNER WARRANTY (HOW)

In order to further look at the future of the home warranty concept, let us investigate a very similar program. The Home Owner Warranty Program (HOW) is a ten year warranty program in use in the new home industry since its inception in 1974. Initiated by the National Association of Home Builders as an industry response to the growing consumer protection movement, its success has been impressive. More than 10,000 builder members of the National Association are now enrolled in the program. As of November, 1978, 400,000 homes were covered by HOW representing $19 billion worth of warranted homes.[22]

Not all builders can offer the warranty program. Each geographic area has a HOW council which screens builder applicants for the necessary credentials. A solid reputation plus adequate financial resources are two of the more important criteria. The HOW Program stipulates that certain quality standards must be met and verified before final approval. Once approved, all homes or condominiums built by a particular HOW builder must be sold with the warranty included in the price. The cost to the builder is an annual membership fee, plus $2.00 per each thousand dollars of sales price on each home sold. It is understood that this fee is passed on to the buyer in the sale price of the home.

In the first year, the builder warrants the structure. Year number two calls for additional warranties by the builder on the heating, cooling, electrical, and plumbing systems. Years three through ten are insured directly by the Insurance Company of North America. The last eight years of coverage are no longer the responsibility of the builder and refer basically to the structural soundness and load bearing ability of the home. The insurance company also has liability in those instances in which the builder goes out of business or cannot otherwise perform the necessary warranty repairs required in the initial two years.

An interesting parallel between the new home warranty and the used home warranties being offered is the reluctance of the builders to embrace this new concept initially. As the new concept began to prove its worth, more and more builders jumped on the bandwagon.

Because of the widespread publicity of the HOW program, many governmental agencies are beginning to require the HOW program or its equivalent on every new home or condominium built within their jurisdiction. As an example, the state of New Jersey enacted legislation requiring the HOW type of warranty on every new home sold in New Jersey after October of 1978.[22] If a warranty program is enjoying such success on brand new homes, does it not appear that the same peace of mind should be available to the buyer of a 40 year old home?

WHO OFFERS WARRANTY SERVICES?

Warranty services are available today from three basic sources. *The greatest number of warranties being sold are those offered by independent warranty companies.* Independent in this connotation refers to those warranty companies not affiliated with a franchise or owned by an individual Realtor firm. The largest independent warranty firm as of March 1979, was American Home Shield of Pleasanton, California. In addition to many large Realtor customers, AHS also has the patronage of some of the national franchises. Offered also on an exclusive basis to select large Realtors in various markets, the AHS warranty program has one other distinction. Coverage on the AHS warranty is extended to cover the seller during the listed period on certain items plus twelve months of buyer protection on more items after the closing. All service requests are handled from Pleasanton, California, by qualified operators over toll free WATS lines.

The second source to offer warranty services are some of the franchise companies. Almost all franchise companies offer a warranty program but this discussion will center on those franchisors who actually own and operate a warranty company themselves. The independent warranty companies will say that a franchisor should not attempt to operate a warranty company because it is a specialized field. They will also say that the franchisor should spend his efforts in franchising and leave the warranty work to them. There may be some truth in that.

From the opposing view, however, it would seem that the franchisor would be doubly aware of the nesessity to make the homeowner happy. After all, the franchisor's royalty income is dependent on the success of each franchisee. Through proper management, the warranty program could be a unique tool on which to build a strong competitive edge for all member franchisees. Extra leniency in the handling of service calls could be expected with a franchisor owned warranty program. This should be true because the franchisor is not totally dependent on warranty income for the necessary profit margin.

The third source of warranty services is those Realtors who underwrite a warranty program on their own. In this group will be found some previous customers of Palace Guard. Palace Guard was the name of the first large national warranty service company. Many fine large Realtor firms were given the service on an exclusive basis in each market.

Because it was a totally new concept, no acturial experience was available to guide Palace Guard in the structuring of the program. Unfortunately, no deductible amount was required to be paid by the home owner on each service call. After being in business for about two years, Palace Guard went out of business in the middle seventies.

This left the participating Realtor with customers who still had time left on their warranty contracts. These brokers stepped in and guaranteed that the services provided on the contracts would continue to be provided by themselves. Some of these same brokers also began selling warranty services to new customers and are continuing to provide warranty coverage to this day. Obviously, the warranty program has more than compensated for the original financial burden placed upon them by the demise of Palace

111

Guard. What is the impact of warranty programs on you, the Realtor?

IMPACT NUMBER 1

A warranty service gives the Realtor his first opportunity to actually enhance the saleability of his product. Think about it. Never before has the Realtor, through his services, been able to add to the value of his product in the eyes of a buyer. Because warranty services are currently available through Realtors, the broker can bring a valuable sales aid to the selling process that a "for sale by owner" cannot provide himself. Now with the warranty service, there is another reason to list with a Realtor.

IMPACT NUMBER 2

Most warranty companies do not offer their programs to every Realtor in each market. This results in a have and have not situation. Those who have a program will, of course, use it in a competitive situation to gain a listing or the loyalty of a buyer.

IMPACT NUMBER 3

Problems are eliminated after the closing for all parties involved. The buyer is taken care of by the warranty company if problems arise with items covered. The seller can go on to his new home safe in the knowledge that his buyer has someone to help him if something goes wrong. This also includes the fact that the buyer will not pursue the seller to demand satisfaction regarding a problem. Lastly, the Realtor and Realtor Associate are now protected after the sale. As they step out of their responsibility to the buyer at closing, the warranty company steps in to continue providing service to the new homeowner.

IMPACT NUMBER 4

The usual Realtor-client relationship is from point of listing to point of closing the sale. Likewise with a buyer, it is from beginning of the search for the right home to the point of closing the sale. Now the service period is extended with a warranty program from the periods just mentioned to twelve months after closing. This new prolonged service period will mean stronger and greater referrals for the Realtor if the warranty work is handled properly. Each service problem handled should provide an opportunity to contact the homeowner to see if he was satisfied with the service and to solicit referrals and or testimonial letters.

IMPACT NUMBER 5

The final impact on the Realtor is that there is now another reason upon which to justify our fees. We are beginning to see increasing attitudes that perhaps the current fee structure is too generous. Some Realtors are offering cut-rate commissions or low flat dollar amounts. Some federal legislators have recommended a mandatory 5% commission rate nationally. A program as worthwhile as the warranty services herein described should help to bolster up the other existing reasons why a Realtor is fairly paid for the services rendered.

OUR
7 CHANGING CLIENTELE

We have talked about new services, competition, and concepts. Let us now turn our attention to the most important subject of all, our customers. Survival in any business is dependent upon the ability to provide goods and services that people want and are willing to pay for. If we can understand our customers, we can respond to their needs and thus assure ourselves continued patronage.

You may read these words and say that the home buyer and seller have not changed. The buyer wants the best home his money can buy on the best terms possible. The seller still wants the same three things: the highest price in the shortest possible time with the least inconvenience. These are still true. However, our clientele is undergoing some subtle changes that we must analyze and accept as realities.

MORE TRANSIENCY

Today's home buyer is much more transient than ever before in our history. This is partially the result of corporate moves.

People are also more restless. One of the prime symptoms of restlessness is the urge to move periodically.

Divorce has become one of the major reasons people sell a home. Once the home is sold and the proceeds split between both parties, two additional possible sales can result.

Lifestyle is a term often used today. People's lifestyle is usually represented by the area they live in and the type of home they own. The young executive moves into the more expensive suburbs as soon as he can and then continues to upgrade himself in size and price as his income rises. The "empty nesters," on the other hand, leave the big home in search of something that does not require the maintenance and upkeep necessary in a large home. Still others seek out particular school systems, proximity to work, and access to transportation. To demonstrate how transient we really are, a statistic was recently offered stating that 88% of all home buyers have already owned one home.

It would appear that increased transiency is probably responsible for more knowledgeable and probably less loyal customers. The obvious knowledge possessed by the average buyer is understandable. Having already bought and sold property, there is no mystery to negotiating, financing, pricing, comparing areas and judging values.

If the buyer is wise in the art of buying and selling real estate, we in the profession of selling real estate must be even better versed in every aspect of a sale. If the prospective customer feels that he or she is more informed than the salesperson, the confidence of the customer can be lost.

Many brokers today feel that their length of service in a community will guarantee their continued success in the future. People are no longer interested in length of service as much as "what have you done for me lately?" Brokers who look to the past may be left in the past. An example of this lack of loyalty can be found in one of the better subdivisions in your area.

You have certainly seen the domination of that subdivision change from one broker to another over a period of time. The company that gets the greatest percentage of business at any one time is the most aggressive company consistently working it. When the leader grows lax or loses the salespeople who served that sub, another broker takes over. Now take this example and apply it to your entire real estate market. The companies offering the best service at a given point in time will be in the leadership positions.

We have spent some time on customer loyalty, because too many brokers do not yet think that they really have to adapt to the new changes around them. For many brokers, life is too comfortable. They have made good money over the years and it doesn't appear that they are in any danger of losing their market position. A word of caution: Don't take past customer loyalties for granted.

IMPACT OF BIGNESS

Nothing has made a more dramatic impact on the buying and selling public than the effective use of mass media by the real estate franchises. With previously-unknown names, the franchises have come to towns across America with clever TV and radio advertising. Beamed directly at the public in the living room on prime time, the image of bigness has been sold to home buyers and sellers as the sign of success.

We Americans have always equated bigness with success. The biggest car, the biggest house, the biggest sales staff, office, ads, and volume are all typical examples. So it appears that the stage is set. Franchise success stories prove that our customers do and will continue to patronize franchised offices in increasing numbers, because they have presented the "big" image through the media.

Now come national real estate brokerage firms that cover the land from coast to coast. Next come multi-million dollar relocation companies with regional offices across

America ready to handle the transferee's needs anywhere in the United States.

You may comment that it doesn't matter how big the competition gets, your firm is still more professional and better equipped to handle customers' needs in your area. You may be right. But your knowing it doesn't make it a fact in the public's mind.

If the franchises and national companies can employ the best ad agencies in the land, their power to persuade will be awesome. You've seen it already. The television advertising used by the franchises has been very powerful. Effective use of mass media can rapidly erode the power base of an oldtime leader in any market. The American public has consistently bought bigness and the apparent success that bigness seems to denote.

INFLUENCE OF CONSUMERISM

Ralph Nader has changed the course of the way business is done. The old "buyer beware" theory is practically gone. The consumer is boss. The American consumer has learned a lot about his rights in a business transaction. Today's customers are more demanding. Under particularly heavy attack is the familiar "as is" clause used on practically all purchase agreements.

Home buyers want someone to turn to if the house needs repairs shortly after they move in. Frankly, brokers should not have to carry the burden of making restitution on homes sold that have problems. But the buyer should not be given the cold shoulder by a broker unwilling to help, either.

Warranty services are the answer. Now a buyer can have someone to turn to when problems arise and the broker can save a lot of money and hassle and still maintain the continuing friendship of past customers. A new home buyer can be warranted for ten years. A new car buyer receives a warranty. The resale home market is next.

The growth of consumerism will mandate the use of warranty programs in the next few years. Don't watch the passing parade. Investigate.

INFLATION AND THE IRS

The single family detached home is the best investment in America! Ask your neighbors to tell you about the best investment they have ever made in their lives. They will tell you that their home was their best decision.

Run away inflation in housing coupled with the 1978 revision in the Internal Revenue Code relating to the sale of a primary residence, and the traditional tax shelters of mortgage interest and property taxes have guaranteed the future of the home as a fantastic investment for a long time to come. The tax reform act of 1978 stipulates that $100,000 in profit may be exempted from capital gains tax on the sale of a primary residence provided that the seller is over age 55, has lived in the home 3 of the previous 5 years, and is not buying another home. Nowhere else can you make an investment, realize a large profit and avoid the taxes on the first $100,000.

Even if the 1978 tax law had not been enacted, however, the buying public today looks upon a home purchase as an investment.

INCREASED KNOWLEDGE NEEDED

We as real estate people must be more knowledgeable as to the amenities that affect home value if we are to advise our customers properly. Location, school system, floor plan, construction, public utilities and services, and other factors contribute to the value of a particular home as a good investment.

Professional use of the computer services available can bring past and current market data out on a teletype machine in seconds. Once the comparables are scrutinized, a financial projection may be printed out showing the tax shelter and equity build up that can be realized on a particular property.

Probably the most investment-minded buyer is the transferee who will be selling his home two or three years after purchase. Many smart transferees have built up their equity rapidly through the wise manner in which they have bought and sold each home as it came time to relocate. Those salespeople working with transferees must be in tune with the market and prepared to properly advise an out of town buyer who will rely on their judgment in deciding on the proper home.

The incentive to purchase a home as a solid investment brings both an opportunity and a responsibility to every person in real estate today. The opportunity, of course, is to be selling a product that serves the basic need of shelter and provides financial well being as a sound investment. The tremendous responsibility this brings is that we must be knowledgeable and accurate in the advise we give our customers. We must know the product we sell. Although our inventory is constantly in a state of change, we should stay in touch with values and trends in each area that affect the resale potential.

Local governmental regulations, changes in zoning ordinances, shifts in property taxes, highway expansion, new shopping centers, school board decisions, new IRS regulations as they relate to home ownership, and other developments all greatly affect the investment potential of any home.

Although we are not tax experts, we have been rather remiss in knowing little about the tax regulations in regard to home ownership. When our customers have inquired about the tax consequences of selling a home, we have told them to reinvest the equity in another home of equal or greater value within eighteen months. This would serve to postpone the capital gains tax on any profit realized from the sale of their home. That information alone doesn't go far enough!

A new record keeping system has been devised that enables every homeowner to know what expenses can and should be recorded so as to minimize the taxable gain on the sale of each home bought and sold. It explains how the tax is figured and how it is postponed from one home purchase to another. Finally, the system describes the four cost categories which include acquisition costs, capital improvements, fix up expenses and selling expenses. The IRS ruling on those moving costs incurred on a job-related move which may be deducted are also detailed. This system could literally save a homeowner thousands of dollars in capital gains taxes over a lifetime of buying and selling homes.

This record keeping system is currently being marketed through select firms across the country. It has proven itself to be a worthwhile service and another good reason to deal with a Realtor.

Our clientele may be changing in other ways not mentioned in this chapter. A few changes have been described here in order to better understand why franchises, national brokerage firms, computer companies, relocation companies, and warranty companies are gaining ground. As our customers change in lifestyle, attitudes, and priorities, so our industry must change with them. Let us, then, not forget the effects of increased transiency, consumerism, the bigness impact, inflation and the IRS on our ever changing clientele.

8 OBSERVATIONS, CONCLUSIONS, ALTERNATIVES

Having looked at new competition, services, trends, and clientele, let us now turn our attention to your brokerage firm as it exists today.

"DAVID AND GOLIATH"

The competitive pressure being created by franchises and emerging national brokerage firms will only make it more difficult for the independent broker in the years ahead. In recent national magazines and newspapers, writers have claimed that perhaps as few as ten large companies will do as much as 80% of the residential brokerage business in the country.[15]

From the Biblical story of "David and Goliath," we can draw a comparison between the independent broker and franchises or national companies. The reality of a very small brokerage firm with 4 or 5 people competing against a large company with 200 salespeople is already commonplace. Add franchised brokers and branch offices of national firms and the scales can really begin to tip in one direction. Continuous use of the mass media and ongoing professional training programs aimed at upgrading both management and sales staff can increase the gap between big and small.

FEE STRUCTURE

A topic barely mentioned in this book is a broker's fee structure. As we all know, every broker is free to determine the proper fee for his or her services. Today, there are various fees charged in most markets by individual companies. Most fees are calculated as a percentage of the sale price of the real estate sold. Because of the inflation in real estate values, these fees continue to increase in actual dollars received. The national brokerage firms now being formed have been asked if they can foresee a change in their fee structure brought on by competition with other giant companies. Their answer has been that they feel the fees will remain the same, and they anticipate offering additional services to their customers.[14] Only future events will show if this forecast is accurate. The competition created between eight or ten national giants could result in some cutting of fees to gain a competitive edge.

If the nationals did reduce fees, it could have a devastating effect on small brokers. Many brokerages are operating with an overhead that is dependent on maintaining the current fee structure. If small competitors would have to respond to lower fees by reducing their own, many could be forced out of business.

A GROWING DEPENDENCY

The real estate brokerage business has always attracted the entrepreneur who seeks to own his business with a relatively small investment in start-up costs. The obvious independence enjoyed in making your own decisions and determining your own destiny have been additional reasons to go in business. In the early 1900's brokers were so independent that they did not even co-operate with other brokers in the sale of property. This practice can still be seen today in some basically rural areas, but to a much smaller degree than before.

Eventually, brokers began to come together in local associations called real estate boards. These boards were, in turn, members of their state association and the National Association of Real Estate Boards (NAREB) that has been renamed The National Association of Realtors (NAR). These local boards were formed primarily to establish rules and regulations whereby the rights of the public and all brokers could be protected by the formation of a code of ethics. Brokers belonging to these boards began to use the registered term "Realtors."

Even though each member had to abide by the rules set up by the local board, everyone still conducted their daily business in a very independent manner. Some would co-operate with some companies and not others. Some would keep their listings a secret while others would invite other brokerages to show their properties and participate in the commission if a buyer was found by a co-operating firm.

The first big innovation, in which the broker became dependent on something outside his own company, was multiple listing. As the power of MLS grew, most companies found that they had to belong in order to have the same advantages as their competitors. This organized method of sharing information has benefited buyers, sellers, and Realtors equally. The advent of the computer in multiple listing has enabled MLS to perform to its optimum capacity.

Membership in a bonafide national referral network is becoming more necessary as our customers become increasingly mobile. Joining such a network will benefit all members in proportion to the effort made by each member. The concept of a national referral, organization like multiple listing, is successful only if there is much co-operation and solidarity with brokers involved. As in MLS, this is another example of a growing dependence on others.

In offering a warranty program, a company depends on the good judgment and fair mindedness displayed by the warranty company in handling customer problems. Some large brokerage firms have underwritten their own warranty programs. Most brokers, however, must turn to an outsider to provide the warranty coverage.

The most outstanding example of dependency has been shown by those firms that have opted for a franchise. They are relying on the talents and expertise of the franchisor to provide the image and services to help their brokerages grow and prosper.

A strong company takes a greater risk in joining a franchise, because it already enjoys some degree of success. Yet, the shrewd broker who is a success as an independent, can become much more so through the proper use of all the things a franchise can offer. The astute broker has learned that giving up some degree of independence can yield a rich harvest in dynamic growth.

ON PURPOSE RATHER THAN BY ACCIDENT

Most brokerage firms are run by accident rather than on purpose! Let's talk about your company. Have you kept records on your performance each year you have been in business? Are you getting a bigger or smaller share of the market? Do you still have control of certain subdivisions as you once did? Have you ever been the dominant broker in any area? Do you, as an owner, have a goal and annual budget planned each year? Do your salespeople have a goal individually?

Equal to having a goal is knowing how they are going to achieve that goal. Do they have a plan? Do you as owner have a plan? Does your existing staff need more training and motivating? How many new people do you need? How many existing people should be cut from the squad? What plan do you have to recruit? How do you conduct an interview? Most brokers end up being interviewed by a prospective salesperson rather than vice-versa. What services and sales aids is your company lacking? When and how will you go about getting them?

The success of a brokerage firm begins and ends with the owner. Those firms that are consistently ahead are led by someone who is goal oriented! They know where they are going and when and how they are going to do it.

We have made easy money in the real estate business! Many firms, some of them mediocre, have thrived in the past few years. They have been spoiled and many have become sloppy in the running of their businesses.

Coming competition and events are going to force us to "get our act together." The times ahead will be the most exciting and revolutionary ever experienced in the real estate brokerage business. These same times will be devastating and traumatic for those who do not respond to our changing times.

PROFILE OF YOUR COMPANY

Have you ever stood back for a moment and analyzed your company? More importantly, have you decided at different intervals the direction you want to take with it? See if your business fits in one of the categories listed below:

—new company looking for credentials
—established firm with consistent growth record
—older firm needing injection of new vitality
—older firm that continually adapts to changes
—leader in your market intent on staying there
—past leader in your market beginning to slip
—number 2 or 3 ready to take on the leader
—large wanting to get larger
—smaller wanting to get larger

127

—smaller wanting to stay small but more profitable and competitive

—large wanting to become more profitable

—typical average brokerage with few services.

Boss Kettering, one of the pioneers with General Motors Corporation, once said, "Any problem once defined is half solved." Maybe you have never looked at your firm in the terms described above. Now is the time to determine the strategies that will make your company strong for many years ahead.

Before we can discuss different alternatives, we must know what you personally want to do. Where do you put yourself in the following list?

YOUR PERSONAL GOALS

—new owner planning to spend your career in this field

—older broker preparing to sell your business

—older broker planning to pass the business on to a family member

—sole proprietor planning to stay that way

—sole proprietor planning to bring in a partner or partners

—owner of a large successful business wanting a buy out by a national firm

—owner of a large firm looking to acquire other firms

—owner exploring franchising

—existing franchisee who is not realizing all the anticipated benefits of franchising

—independent broker wanting to keep one office but expand staff

—one office owner wanting to open additional branch or branches.

The proper direction for your business is the one that enables you to accomplish your own personal goals. A strong and vibrant business can help you achieve any goal you have in mind.

Many brokers plan on leaving their business to a family member or a valued member of their current staff. The challenges faced by the departing owner were much different than those that must be faced by the new owner. Proper planning now can give the new owner a strong track to run on.

WHY SHOULD SOMEONE COME TO WORK FOR YOUR COMPANY?

A business's success or failure can be determined by the quality of the people involved in the organization. Everyone wants good people, but not all companies offer the same potential for a sales associate. An objective way to analyze your brokerage firm is to answer the question stated above. What do you have to offer a career minded sales associate? Why should a good person work with your firm instead of your competitor? Is your company structured with strong management and sound programs designed to help a sales associate operate at maximum capacity?

Some of the below listed items are found in every successful brokerage firm. Which ones apply to your company?

ATTRIBUTES OF A SUCCESSFUL COMPANY

—experienced and goal-oriented management
—regular and ongoing recruiting program
—professional interviewing and screening process
—effective initial training program
—continual training and refresher programs
—good compensation plan with built-in incentives to achieve
—good office location with ample identification
—functional office layout and decor
—ongoing motivation and recognition of achievers

—business atmosphere denoting a sense of urgency
—standard rules applied equally to all
—good public image
—consistent, professional advertising policies
—national connections through referral organization
—decisive management seeking excellence, impatient with mediocrity
—professional administrative and secretarial staff
—open dialogue between management and sales associates.

There are other criteria not listed herein. All of these features can enable you to attract and maintain good people in your organization. Review the items on this list and see how your business compares.

AUTHOR'S CONCLUSIONS

The author has tried to outline and detail as many facts as possible about all the changes that are taking place in the real estate business. He will now list some of his conclusions from his point of view:

Conclusion No. 1
The real estate brokerage business will undergo greater changes in the 1980s than ever seen before.

Conclusion No. 2
The irreversible trend toward bigness will increase in momentum.

Conclusion No. 3
The greatest force of change will be the national real estate brokerage firms.

Conclusion No. 4
Many average and marginal firms will be unable to compete for good people and will go out of business.

Conclusion No. 5

Relocation companies will continue to penetrate the transferee market and virtually control a large volume of good listings nationally.

Conclusion No. 6

Franchises will increasingly appeal to better brokerage firms who want to run their own business and compete effectively with the national firms.

Conclusion No. 7

Home warranties will be as numerous as title insurance policies.

Conclusion No. 8

Computer companies will continue to expand the number of services available, thus becoming an integral part of every modern real estate office.

Conclusion No. 9

Better educated and more professional people will be attracted into real estate sales as a career. The majority of these will gravitate toward the national companies and franchises.

Conclusion No. 10

Independents and franchisees will have to run their businesses in a much more professional and business-like manner in order to keep up with the national firms.

Conclusion No. 11

The growing national firms and franchises will account for the majority of residential resale business written.

The conclusions listed above are those of the author and are opinions formed over a period of time working in different real estate related businesses and from gathering the research material for this book. In reviewing the facts presented throughout this book, you may have come to different conclusions. These differences are certainly healthy and most welcome.

ALTERNATIVES

As we look down the road into the 1980's, it appears certain that every broker who is currently non-aligned with franchises or national companies will be facing one of the following alternatives:

REMAIN INDEPENDENT

The easiest decision for any broker is to remain as he or she is now, independent. Having been successful thus far, it would appear that there is no reason to change. No one now knows what kind of independent company will be able to exist in a business dominated by national firms and franchises. It seems fair to say that many independents will survive.

Many of the large multi-branch companies will be purchased by the national companies. They are prime targets for the national firm that is seeking market supremacy in each area. The current trends in those companies being acquired shows us that this is true. Some of these large companies are also banding together in franchises with other strong firms.

It seems, then, that those companies remaining independent are primarily one office firms. Those one office firms that currently are leaders in their local areas are more reluctant to join franchises. Those seeking to pass up the leaders are buying franchises as a tool to gain the upper hand.

Perhaps the independent most likely to succeed is the firm that is small serving a small market. The strong personal following enjoyed in a small community may provide the necessary margin of success for an independent. As the market area grows larger and more impersonal, this loyal patronage begins to be eroded by those presenting a bigger image.

If the overhead can be kept down and recruiting new

people is not important, a small independent could probably hold on for a long time. Any attempt to compete with the giants in advertising, training, referrals, and other services would be foolhardy. Personal contact and involvement in the community will be the primary source of business.

An obvious advantage of remaining independent is the satisfaction of keeping all your options open. More important to many brokers is the ability to keep their own separate identity free of any affiliation with anyone else.

Many real estate companies have been built on the personality of the founder of the firm. This personality has made an impact on the local community and has successfully provided the leadership to attract business and salespeople. Many independents do have difficulty when the leadership changes to a new generation. If the new owner does not also possess strong leadership traits, the organization can disintegrate through the combination of new ownership and insufficient credentials to hold good people. How many times have you seen a good company falter after the departure of the originator?

Being independent puts a burden on the broker who really wants to have a strong company. Every service and innovation must be initiated by the owner acting alone. With no one to consult or act as a sounding board, the owner will structure a business that basically reflects his views and ambition or lack of ambition.

If you are still an independent broker, you may feel that remaining so does not cost you anything. It may be costing you a lot of additional business that you could be enjoying! There is a cost in remaining independent! Whatever your inclination may be, investigate the new realities mentioned in this book. National firms, franchises, relocation companies, warranty companies, and computer companies are all having an increasing impact on the way homes are bought and sold in America. Be informed. Don't let the rapidly changing events catch you unaware.

SELECT A FRANCHISE

Another alternative available is franchising. Accord'ng to the National Association of Realtors, the brokers owning a franchise have doubled from 8.5% of the membership to 17% in the last three years.[17] Many franchises are already taken for certain areas. As mentioned in earlier chapters, the type of company joining franchises is continuing to improve. A broker who can run an office successfully as an independent, could really utilize the additional services provided by a franchise affiliation. Some of the criteria to use in assessing a franchise are:

- —quality of franchisor personnel
- —quality of franchisees in your area
- —depth of services
- —the size of exclusive area allowed (not too small or too large)
- —ability to follow through on promises made
- —success versus failure ratio (gone out of business or left franchise)
- —training program and its implementation
- —national referral network
- —accessibility of franchisor staff
- —warranty program and how it works
- —corporate relocation division
- —financial strength
- —number of existing offices
- —terms of its contract
- —quality of image and easy recognition by general public.

It is the author's firm belief that national real estate firms will provide the greatest threat to the small brokerage firm. Buying a franchise will be the same as buying life insurance! You will still continue to own and operate your business. Yet, you will be able to provide first rate services to attract sales personnel and customers.

Strength in numbers is a concept that has come of age in the real estate business. Many companies working together under one identity can achieve much more than working alone. The public is being sold on the advantages of bigness. *Franchises offer the image of bigness and the autonomy of individual ownership.*

Most franchises are sold through the master franchise concept. This plan calls for the sale of a whole state to one individual. This individual then sells separate franchises to brokers in his state only. Most franchises have varying degrees of success in different states depending on the capabilities of the master franchisor in each state. Be sure to check out the support staff and training organization employed by the master franchisor in your state.

Most salespeople are thrilled to learn that their broker decided to join a franchise. They certainly have noticed the ads on TV and the general inroads being made by franchises in their areas. The best way to announce your decision to franchise is on an individual basis with each salesperson. This gives them the opportunity to understand your decision and the reasons for it. It also prevents them from being intimidated by some negative person in the organization who could make a damaging impact if it was announced to all at a sales meeting. The most valuable people should be told first.

If you have made up your mind to franchise, be decisive in your attitude and put your best efforts into implementing the new programs immediately. The salespeople will probably look to you for leadership. If you are positive about the franchise decision, it can give an injection of new enthusiasm to your entire organization. Not all salespeople may agree with your decision. Some will want to wait and see how it goes. Remember that salespeople do not always have the same priorities as the owner.

The owner is concerned about the value of his business in the future, ability to recruit good people, and the constant upgrading of his competitive status as new forces continue to change the marketplace. Once you implement a franchise, use as many of its services as you can. Learn about everything that is offered. Be sure that you are getting your money's worth. Use the training for your people as well as yourself. Management training is just as important for the owner as sales training is for the sales staff. No one knows everything there is to know about managing and motivating a sales staff. Goal setting and budgeting is another area that is notoriously weak in the brokerage business. Make inquiries about the franchise opportunities available to you. Whether you buy or not, do yourself the favor of being fully informed.

ACQUIRE OR BE ACQUIRED

Some brokers are buying out existing companies to become stronger in their immediate market. Still others are purchasing companies in distant areas, thus opening up new areas of penetration. If the funds are available, this can certainly facilitate a rapid growth rate. The national firms like Coldwell Banker and Merrill Lynch are looking for the biggest firms available. Some acquisitions are being made of midsize companies by other brokers. Most companies being bought are primarily one office firms where a retiring broker is selling out to a larger firm looking for branches in additional areas.

The company doing the buying usually prefers to engage the selling broker in an employment contract thus assuring continuity of management. It gives the selling party some dollars plus a guaranteed buyer for the business based upon an agreed formula.

Some of the advantages of selling out include a potential rejuvenation by becoming part of a larger entity, increased recognition in the community, a guaranteed financial arrangement, and opportunity for growth if the selling party does not plan to leave the business.

In the formula proposed by Merrill Lynch, the selling party would maintain a 20% interest in the company. If the anticipated growth takes place, the 20% partial ownership could be worth more than the sales price of the original 80% portion.

The national companies are looking to acquire those firms that are large, profitable, and possessing good management. The tendency of a firm having these qualities, is to go it alone. The national company has to be convincing that it is beneficial for the target company to sell out. The firms acquired by Coldwell Banker seem to have benefitted from the new association. It also appears to be the policy of Coldwell Banker to give the acquired company considerable autonomy over its own affairs.

Size is not the only feature that determines if a purchase is desirable. The profitability of a company is extremely important. Size is not proof that a particular firm is profitable. In fact, many large firms are not nearly as profitable as they should be. These national companies are responsible to their stockholders for making profits. They can be counted on to weigh the profitability of a company heavily in determining whether to buy and/or what price to offer. If you are inclined to sell your business in the future, take a hard look at that bottom line. Your buyer sure will!

SUMMARY

This book has been compiled in an effort to draw together all the forces at work in today's brokerage business. Facts and opinions have been presented. Most working brokers are really not aware of all these new dynamics and their potential impacts.

Look at yourself and your business! Know what is happening in your industry! Prepare for the Real Estate Revolution! Good Luck!

REFERENCES

1. "Canadian Real Estate—1979," *The A. E. LePage Market Survey,* A. E. LePage, Ltd., 1978
2. *1978 Real Estate Survey, Ontario* A. E. LePage, Ltd. 1977
3. Press release entitled, "A. E. LePage Purchases Assets of Toronto's Second Largest Real Estate Broker," A. E. LePage, Ltd., November 9, 1978
4. *The Achievers in Commercial and Residential Real Estate,* A. E. LePage, Ltd.
5. "LePage's Investment in U.S. Real Estate Culminates 65 Years of Steady Growth," *The Globe and Mail,* August 27, 1977
6. "Giants Joined," *A. E. LePage Coast to Coast Real Estate Service News,* Vol. 5, No. 2
7. "Why George Babbit Should be Smiling in His Grave," *Forbes,* September 4, 1978
8. *Coldwell Banker Annual Report, fiscal year 1978*
9. "Reviving the Business of Home Warranties," *Business Week,* March 5, 1979

10. "Courting the Third Party Company," *Real Estate Today,* January, 1978, Vol. 11, No. 1
11. *The Leading Personnel Relocation Management Service Company,* Homequity, Inc.
12. *RRS, We Find Ways to Help,* Relocation Realty Service Corp.
13. "Coldwell Banker Announces Acquisition of Barton and Ludwig," *Nationwide News,* January, 1979
14. "Why Merrill Lynch Wants to Sell Your House," *Fortune,* January 29 1979
15. "Corporate Giants Invade the Residential Market," *New York Times*
16. *Proceedings of Relocation Management, '78,* Merrill Lynch Relocation Management, Inc., 1978
17. *Membership Profile 1978,* National Association of Realtors, 1978
18. *A Study of Employee Relocation Policies Among Major U.S. Corporations 1978,* Merrill Lynch Relocation Management, Inc., 1978
19. "Member Profile of the National Association of Realtors," *Real Estate Status Report,* National Association of Realtors, September, 1978
20. "Merrill Lynch Holds Talks to Acquire Control of 10 Realty Brokerage Firms," *The Wall Street Journal,* September 22, 1978
21. Western Union Mailgram, Nationwide Relocation Service, Inc., dated July 26, 1978.
22. "Warranty Saves Wear and Tear," *Detroit Free Press,* November 18, 1978
23. *Webster's New Collegiate Dictionary,* 1961

83
85
88